Rule the Freakin' Markets

How to Profit in Any Market, Bull or Bear

Michael Parness

St. Martin's Griffin ☙ New York

www.stmartins.com

LIBRARY OF CONGRESS CATALOGING-IN-PUBLICATION DATA

Parness, Michael.
    Rule the freakin' markets : how to profit in any market, bull or bear / Michael Parness.
        p. cm.
    ISBN 0-312-28256-7 (hc)
    ISBN 0-312-30307-6 (pbk)
    EAN 978-0312-30307-5
    1. Stocks. 2. Speculation. 3. Investments. 4. Investment analysis. I. Title.

    HG6041 .P297 2002
    332.63'22—dc21

                                                            2001048874

10   9   8   7   6   5   4   3   2

Contents

Contents

Acknowledgments

Many people contributed to the writing of this book in a multitude of ways, both large and small. First and foremost I thank Kirstin Peterson for her indispensable assistance in the writing of this book. My agent, Nick Ellison, was instrumental in shepherding the entire project through the publication process. At St. Martin's Press, my editor, George Witte, was a great source of enthusiasm and was always open to new ideas. His assistant, Marie Estrada, was also great to work with.

For their help with charts and other technical matters, I'm grateful to Tiny (Michael Saul), Nikola Ivanov, and Merrick Okamoto. Tiny also provided me with invaluable time to help put the book together by more than adequately running the TrendFund.com chat room. Thanks also to my staff at TrendFund.com for being a constant source of strength and integrity in the marketplace. You rock!

Early readers of the book proposal include Amy Gutman, Eric Peterson, and Mary Peterson; their suggestions helped make it stronger. I am indebted to my publicist, Michael Sietz-Honig, for a hundred kinds of help that I can never recount. Finally, I'd like to acknowledge all the traders on **www.trendfund.com** for showing me how to help them *Rule the Freakin' Markets*!

Foreword

It's been several years now since I wrote *Rule the Freakin' Markets*. The hardcover has gone through several printings, and the book has been translated into at least six different languages, and is a *Wall Street Journal* bestseller to boot. It's also been several years since I turned a few thousand dollars into *many* millions of them as a *trend trader*. As with anything else in life, I've learned a lot since I started trading, and I've learned even more since I wrote this book you now have in your hands. Learning a lot means making a lot of mistakes. For a trader to *net* millions of dollars, that means he/she also lost millions of dollars to get there. No trader makes money on every trade, and no trader doesn't lose money on a *lot* of trades. It's the nature of the beast. It's been statistically shown that a good trader only needs to "hit" on 40 percent of their trades to be successful. I hope that concepts in this book lead you, as they have led many others, to a much higher "hit" rate, and thus a bigger bank account.

I've been asked many times at seminars over the last few years if I could now, in today's market, turn roughly $33,000 into over $7,000,000 in less than two years. My answer is simple and emphatic—No! Or, despite my belief that anything is possible—probably not! The market, admittedly, is *very* different today than it was when I turned what was left of my savings into a fortune. Further, I don't trade that much anymore; my life as a trader is now about being a teacher and motivator. However, I also preface that answer by saying that I believe it is possible to become a multimillionaire trading stocks using the methods we teach and preach at Trendfund.com *if* you are disciplined and you work at it.

Depending on what you start with, the time it might take you varies. We have several clients who have made millions trading with us, so I know it's possible. We recently had a documented case of a client turning $5,000 into $50,000 in a week, so certainly it's possible for *you* to achieve all the success you want as a trader, and in life.

When I started trading my only goal was to get back the money I lost with a broker, who had made me broke. My "dream" was to get back the $150,000 or so he cost me. If I had just done that I'd have shortchanged myself. Don't do that to yourself. Set your goals high—realistic, but high. This book is meant as a primer to get you started, it's not meant as a cure-all, end all for trading. The examples given are generic because I want the book to last forever. My good friend and comrade at Trendfund.com, Tiny, always says that the market is a living and breathing animal. He thinks it's alive (I don't, but I like the analogy), and always changing. To be a successful trader *you* must always be ready and *willing* to change to a new market environment. If you are stuck on what you do, you will fail. Think about all the great investors in history. Think about all the great companies throughout history. The ones that succeeded are the ones who adapted to change and expanded upon it. In the 1920s during the next great "boom," the hottest stocks were the railroads. At one point *bowling alleys* were seen as the next best thing. Do you want to invest in a few bowling alleys? Or in the railroad stocks? One of the greatest things about being a trader is that you don't ever have to be *right* for the long haul, just for today or for the next month at most. You don't have to think about what the next *big* thing is, *you* are the next best thing . . . if you apply yourself.

When I started trading there were maybe 500,000 traders. After the dot-com bust in 2000 that number busted as well. Estimates ranged from 150,000 to 300,000 or so. That's because most traders could not adapt to going *short* (you'll learn about making money when the market goes *down* later in the book, it's easy!), they only knew that AMZN (Amazon), EBAY, and ETYS (E-Toys, which no longer exists!) would always go *up*! They were wrong, and most of those who made a mint when the market went straight *up* lost it *all* and often *more* when it crashed! I didn't! That's why I got to write this book, and why *you* should read it!

Also, the number of traders has steadily increased. *My Trend Trading to Win* infomercial package has sold over 150,000 units to date and sells roughly 5,000 new clients each and every month! Not all of them end up big winners, and some end up losers, but the fact that the market is no longer the province of institutional investors is a *very* good thing. By definition a market means you should be able to profit from it whether it goes *up* or *down*. That's what we do and that's what *Rule the Freakin' Markets* proposes to help you learn.

As a primer for your journey as a trader, I am proud to offer you these pages. I've heard it said to take what you need and leave the rest behind in life and you will go far. Trading is many things. For me it has provided freedom beyond my wildest dreams. Last year I made one of my dreams come true. I wrote and directed my first feature film—*Max and Grace* (www.maxandgrace.com). I've had my life story optioned and I've been honored at the United Nations for my charity work with children. Trading made it all possible, and my clients have made my life as a trader worthwhile. I am grateful for them all, and I am grateful you have chosen to start your career, or continue it, using my book as a light to guide you.

Keep your goals in mind, and always be truthful to yourself and you cannot fail. Whether you become a greater trader than I am, or you decide *Ruling the Freakin' Markets* isn't for you, you've taken a step forward, and in life taking a step is *always* a good thing, and always leads you to your destiny, a destiny of your choosing.

See ya on the other side,
Michael "Waxie" Parness

Part I

Preparing to Win

....

It's Time to Rule
the Freakin' Markets!

....

In January 1999, I started trading online with, as best I can figure, around $33,000. It was all I had left after blind faith in a broker's advice lost almost 80 percent of my money in six months. That loss hurt, and I was fighting mad. I wanted my money back, and I was going to get it—by myself, whatever it took, without *anybody's* help.

I devoted myself to learning what makes stock prices move. I began to pick stocks and trade by myself. I pondered the mass psychology that moves the market. And gradually, I learned how that psychology drives powerful market trends that repeat themselves again and again. I made money, made mistakes, learned from them, and became better and better at the game. *And, believe me, the stock market is a game.*

After just over a year of full-time trading, my modest account grew into many millions of dollars. That's a return of *thousands* of percent. And I continued to make money—consistently—as the Internet bubble deflated, and afterward while the market tried to find a new direction.

That's a lot of ka-chingos, baby!

How was this possible? What's the secret? How can *you* succeed in the stock market, hoovering up profits while protecting your gains from quick immolation when the market turns south?

There's no Holy Grail in trading, no one secret or "system" that will make you instantly and forever successful in the market. But there are a few simple principles that make all the difference between success and failure in trading. By following those principles, keeping an open mind, and learning from experience, you will become a more intelligent, capable, consistent trader with the finely tuned judgment that will help you make the most of market opportunities. Your goal is to break the bad habits that have kept you from *letting the market work for you*. By opening this book, you're taking your first big step toward improving your trading skills and your financial situation.

■ ■ ■

Maybe you're thinking, *Hey, dude, glad you've done so well, but nothing that good will ever happen to me because I'm genetically programmed to lose money. Every investment I've ever made has been a loser. I've started telling my friends to sell what I buy and buy what I sell, and they're making money. Besides, to succeed in the market you have to be a Wall Street insider or just plain lucky, because for us little guys it's nothing more than a crapshoot. Some people get lucky—like my neighbor's teenager, who got herself a red Miata trading Internet stocks during the crazy bull market. But that will never happen to me, because I'm not an insider and I'm not lucky.*

Here's what I have to say to you: I used to be a losing trader, too. My first attempts to make money in the stock market were the ultimate train wreck. Ready, set, crash and burn. I was truly Mr. Loser. I had a lot to learn—not only how to make money, but how to keep it from disappearing in a falling market. But I did learn—how to make the market work for me, how to beat the Wall Street pros at their own game, and ultimately, how to *rule the freakin' market*! I like to think of it as a form of martial art, where a well-trained hundred-pound fighter can shift his weight to take down a three-hundred-pound brute.

The market may be a ten-thousand-pound brute, but so much the better!

As for being lucky, well, luck has nothing to do with market success because *the market is not a casino*. It's a test of knowledge, self-control, and patience, a game where realists win and gamblers lose. What you need to succeed are the desire and the will to make yourself into the kind of trader that plays to win, and the openness and discipline for constant learning.

The story of how I went from Mr. Loser to successful trader has given many people faith that the American Dream is still alive and well. You don't have to be anyone special to succeed in the market. I sure wasn't. I'm a filmmaker and playwright, not a Harvard M.B.A. or Wall Street suit.

Let me tell you about my journey from zero to hero.

I grew up in Queens, New York. My family was always barely scraping by—my stepfather drove a cab, worked in sales, and did stand-up comedy (an art at which he was not hugely gifted). More than once, paper IOUs were all my sisters and brother and I got for Christmas. I had knives pulled on me more than once when I was in my teens, and I even spent some time living on the streets, homeless.

Life and my own financial experiments taught me some early lessons about how *not* to manage money, and how to avoid getting rich. When I was twelve, I spent a lot of time at the racetrack. My bookie, a guy called Fernie, made quite a lot off of me, but I was one stubborn loser. I hung out at the track throughout high school, always hoping for that one big, big win but for some reason never managing to get it. I even bought a bunch of penny stocks when I was nineteen, about $2,500 worth, and ended up losing it all.

I did learn a few things about how to make money, though. When I was in my teens, I had every odd job you can think of—delivering Chinese food, driving a taxi, working as a security guard. I also started a business selling comic books, which turned out to be a great success. I ran booths in all the big comic-book exhibitions at

New York City hotels, and through my business I began to learn the practical psychology of a market.

I couldn't apply that knowledge to the stock market, though, because I didn't yet realize that stocks are basically the same game. Even if I had, it wouldn't have mattered much. At the time, online trading didn't exist. The only way to invest was through a traditional broker.

When I was in my early twenties, I tried to invest again, this time with a "respectable" broker. I bought a bunch of stocks and proceeded to watch them. I had no control over my investment, and could only watch it slowly wither away. Once again, I lost all my money. Feeling like an outsider who'd been taken for another ride, I decided to forget about the stock market.

Eventually, I decided to pursue my lifetime dream of becoming a playwright and screenwriter. The mean streets of my childhood make for some great stories, and I wanted to tell them all. I moved to Manhattan and became a bartender, since that's what starving artist types in New York City do to get by. Well, I mixed drinks for *quite* a few years, all over New York, and worked as a bouncer in after-hours clubs (the ones that open at 4 A.M. and close again at noon) and wrote plays and struggled and starved. I was even homeless again for a while, when there was finally no more rent money and I spent months going from one friend's couch to another. I felt like I would never amount to anything. I wanted to stop trying, but the street kid in me wouldn't give up.

Then, about ten years ago, when I was still tending bar, I read a *New York Times* article about how valuable old baseball cards had become, and how a Mike Schmidt rookie card was worth five hundred dollars. The baseball-card market was hot, like the stock market was recently. By some miracle, my mom had never thrown out my old collection, and I sold my cards for a nice chunk of change.

But that wasn't good enough. I'm a curious, determined kind of guy, and I wanted to figure out how this hot market worked and how it could become a business. I wanted to learn whatever the world had to teach me. I scraped together some money from my brother and started a business selling baseball cards and sports memorabilia. My specialty was unopened packages of cards, old wax packs from the seventies. I became the Waxman, later Waxie, and I learned more and more about how changes in context can give an object greater value to a buyer. I don't mean only things like the physical condition of a card, but things like whether the player was being sent to the Hall of Fame that year, or being considered for the Cy Young Award, or about to break this or that all-time record.

Eventually the business became my full-time job, to the point where, after eight years or so, Waxman Inc. was one of the biggest baseball-card dealerships in the country. Life was looking pretty darn peachy.

I was feeling so good that, even with all my bad experiences, I decided it was time to invest in the stock market again.

As luck would have it (not good luck, as it turned out), I had a friend who was a stockbroker. I decided to invest my nest egg of about $150,000 in the stock market. My friend the broker told me which stocks to buy, and I bought them. What could be easier? I was an investor, buying stocks to hold indefinitely with no plan. Some of the stocks were penny stocks. Initially they all went up, and I thought, *This is great!* But in reality, they were all pretty bad stocks, and when you start out with little pieces of doodie, that's what they're always going to be in the end. Gradually, all my stocks started to go down, down, down.

It was pretty depressing. On top of that, I had started to dismantle my baseball-card business because I'd decided it was time to move on. It was time for me to get back to writing and making films. I had planned to live on my savings and on the profits I would make in the stock market.

Things didn't turn out quite as I'd planned.

That's how, not long ago, I found myself living in a dingy closet of an apartment in Manhattan for about $550 a month. If you know anything about New York apartment rents, you'll know that's about as low as you can go before hitting the street. If that weren't bad enough, I started reading in the newspaper that the Dow and NASDAQ were making new highs day after day. I asked myself, *Why are my stocks doing nothing while everybody else is getting rich?*

Then came the dramatic market bottom of October 1998. Before the market tanked, although my stocks had lost me a lot of money, at least they'd been worth *something*. After the tankage, I was really wiped out. One of the companies disappeared. Another was delisted. One truly loathsome stock had gone from thirty dollars to four dollars per share. The rest just kept going down. Even now, those smelly little stocks have not come back. As for my broker, let's just say that he's not my friend anymore.

I had lost nearly 80 percent of my investment in less than six months. After the market tanked, I gave up on it for a while because it all seemed so pointless. I stopped watching CNBC. I turned away from its king of coiffure, Joe Kernan, and even forsook my favorite, the lovely Money Honey herself, Maria Bartiromo. All I could do was curl up in a corner and lick my wounds.

It was weeks before I emerged from my dark little cave. I stepped into the light of day, blinked, and found that the market had rallied again. The NASDAQ was hitting new highs.

At the time, all that was left of my 150,000-dollar investment was about $33,000. My stocks lay in my account like corpses after a war. I felt like just about everyone does when they lose money: I felt like a loser. I felt like I would never succeed at anything ever again. I felt like I *really sucked*, fundamentally, as a human being.

But, more importantly, it became clear to me that *someone had taken my money*. And where I come from, if you take my money, *I'm gonna take something from you!* I really started to get mad. I said to myself, *I'm gonna figure out how to get my money back!*

So I started to do a little reading, subscribed to some free information services, and began to figure out why this terrible thing had happened and how to get my money back.

I sold some of my bad stocks for a few thousand dollars and opened an account with an online broker. The first thing I did was to buy four option calls on AOL because it was a highflier that was going up every single day. If the stock kept going up, my options would make money. One day soon after that, I saw that AOL had gone up by ten or fifteen points. I didn't know exactly what was driving AOL up, but I knew that I was making money. The very same thing happened the next day. *Ka-chingo!* It was a classic AOL run, the kind that used to happen pretty often. I decided that I needed to figure out *why* this run was happening.

Feeling more optimistic, I read an article about how Data Broadcasting, an Internet company, was going to spin off CBS Marketwatch as a separate company. I figured that doing this must be worth quite a lot to Data Broadcasting, the parent company. Then I saw that Delia's, another Internet, was also spinning off part of itself, iTurf. I sold what was left of the stinky stocks in my old brokerage account and bought those two parent stocks. A few weeks after I bought them, their prices had more than doubled. *Wowsa!* I was ecstatic.

At this point, I started to think, *I know what I'm doing!* And, *Brokers are a menace to society!* At least I was right on the second point. As for the first one, well, I found out that I still had a lot to learn. But the important thing was that I began to think seriously about *how things work in the market.* I'm not mechanical, and I'm not good at figuring out technical stuff like computers or plumbing or chain saws, but I can figure out how things measure up in terms of probability. And probability is what trading is all about.

I started to do a lot of research to find other Internet companies that were spinning off parts of themselves, and I found some others and played them. I started to perfect the play, to try to figure out the absolute best times to get in and get out of positions (to the extent you can figure out the absolute best *anything* in the market).

I also started to think that, if this particular play was working practically all the time, there must be other things that worked as consistently. Of course, there is *nothing* in the market, or in life, that works 100% of the time, but you don't need to be right about *everything* to make a lot of money if you stay nimble and limit your losses on the things you're wrong about. Think of it this way: Even if you're right only 60 percent of the time, and your upside is 15 percent and you limit your downside to 7 percent, *you have to make money*. Realistically, though, I've found that it's possible for me to be right much more often—around 80 percent of the time—and that the upside of many plays is far, *far* more than 15 percent. In a bull market, it can be anywhere from 10 percent to 400 percent on swing trades, and even more than that in some cases. In a bear market, it can be from 5 percent to 100 percent, and even more for options.

So there I was, making money on stocks by doing my own research and making my own decisions. By early April, I had made a few hundred thousand dollars from my $33,000 and was starting to develop a pleasant feeling of invincibility: *I rule the freakin' markets! I can't lose!* You've probably had that feeling yourself, at least for a day or an hour or a few minutes. Of course, everyone's a genius when the market is going up every single day, as it was at the time. People start believing that it won't ever go down. And that's a *very* good sign that the market is nearing its top.

Sure enough, soon after that moment of invincibility came the April correction. Now, corrections are actually a good and healthy thing for the market. If a market just went straight up for months and never pulled back, it would become so unstable that eventually it would come crashing down all at once in a blazing pile of ticker tape. Instead, it goes up for a while, then pulls back a bit to prepare itself for the next leg up. Corrections are expected in a healthy market, and we have to anticipate them and use them to our advantage. Besides, isn't it true that if everything in life were good every day, we wouldn't really know what goodness is?

But in April 1999, I hadn't yet learned to make money when the market was tanking. I had come back to the market at a good time the previous January—it was near its bottom, and just starting on a real upward tear. I had made good money. And when the correction came, I gave back just about all of it. The things that work in a bull run don't work in a correction. You can have the greatest stock in the world, but chances are good that in a correction it will get beaten down along with everything else.

The funny thing was that I had been pretty sure a correction was coming. I had read that Internet stocks usually sell off after earnings are reported in March and early April, so it seemed likely that this was when the market would correct. But I didn't know what to do about it. I just held on to my stocks and watched them go down and thought, *Wow, I really suck.* I didn't sell any stocks short—sell borrowed stocks at a high price, with the intent to buy and return them when the price had gone down—because I was afraid. I had heard that you could lose everything selling short—*the house, the kids, and the puppy dog!* I still had to acquire one of the basic tools we all need to be able to profit in any market.

So now it was time to figure out how to *make* money in a correction, and even in what investors dread most—a bear market. Starting out with small trades, I taught myself to sell short. I also began to strictly limit my losses when *any* trade didn't go my way. And I continued to learn everything I could about the market's behavior. I watched CNBC, researched companies, and looked for patterns that could help me understand why traders reacted the way they did to news, economic data, and technical factors in the market. I exchanged ideas with other traders and put in lots of late nights. Once the market started to go back up again, I made my money back and then some. Three months later, when the July 1999 correction came, I was better prepared and actually made money during the downdraft by selling short. I've done well in bear markets ever since, and found the big 2000 and 2001 technology stock meltdowns to be amazing trading opportunities.

Now I can make money and preserve profits in *any* market. If you want to make money during good days and bad, or at least keep what's yours, you must learn to use the same techniques.

■ ■ ■

By opening this book, you've taken the first step toward becoming a profitable trader. As in any quest to improve your situation, just showing up is half the battle. The other half is laid out in the chapters that follow. In these chapters, I'll show you how to become a better trader or investor by reevaluating your strategy, finding a comfortable style, understanding the psychology of the market, and overcoming the psychological Achilles' heels that cause you to make money-losing decisions. I'll show you good and bad approaches to picking stocks, how to play a stock successfully from start to finish, and how to make money when the market turns bearish. You'll learn the money-management techniques that are the single most important aspect of trading, and how to recover in the event of a large loss. Finally, I'll show you that stock trading and financial success aren't ends in themselves, but should be the means to other ends that truly enrich your life. To me, everything we do in life should be about realizing our dreams, financial or otherwise.

This book is for beginning traders and investors as well as those with more experience who need to step back and rework their approach. If you have some stock-trading experience, this book may contain principles and information that you have heard before. That's fine. I have worked with traders and investors at all levels, and have seen even people with lots of experience consistently make certain common mistakes. Many have been helped by having basic principles set out clearly and reinforced over and over again. It's human nature for people to do things they shouldn't even when they know better. This is why analyzing your own psychological tendencies is so valuable. To trade or invest successfully, you must have the basic rules firmly in mind and follow them consistently.

Paul Newman once said that he became who he is by accepting the gifts that were offered to him. The market has incredible gifts to give, if you're prepared to take them. The market can also wipe you out in a matter of days if you let it, and it won't ever say it's sorry. You may have lost money in the market already, and may have opened this book to learn how to improve your trading ability. In these pages, I'll show you how to prepare yourself intellectually, psychologically, and emotionally to receive the eye-popping profits the stock market offers. I'll teach you to trade successfully while avoiding the pitfalls that I and many others have encountered while doing battle with Wall Street professionals, chat-room manipulators, and plain old panicky investors. Whether you have three thousand dollars or three million, I will teach you to *play to win*.

Trading is hard work. It requires discipline, patience, flexibility, an open mind, and a commitment to learning every day. But the rewards can be great for those who have the discipline to trade in a consistently safe and responsible way. For me, the greatest reward in trading has come from helping those of limited means who a few years ago were shut out of the market by high brokers' fees. Although the market still is not a truly level playing field, there is now a chance for traders with small accounts to enjoy the rewards that until recently were reserved for market professionals and large investors.

See you on the other side!

Chapter 1

The Knucklehead Within

Identifying Your Type

This chapter covers:
- Why everyone is vulnerable to self-defeating behavior
- Common types of self-defeating and risky behavior
- Why you must recognize your own inner knucklehead
- How to control your inner knucklehead and become a successful trader

Your Inner Knucklehead Wants You to Lose Money

Sigmund Freud said that deep down inside, everyone has a secret death wish. It's the same with trading stocks. Everyone, deep down inside, has a financial death wish. The difference between winners and losers is how well they control it.

Would Freud have made a great stock trader? I don't know for sure, but I think he might have. Everything about the market makes *way* more sense if you look at it in terms of human nature and psychology. (Some days it's tempting to think there's some kind of *abnormal* psychology involved, some kind of mass delusion or psychosis, but it's actually much simpler than that.) Anyone on Wall Street will tell you that the market is driven by only two things—greed and fear—and, on a grand scale, the power of traders' self-interest really does control the market.

But not everything investors and traders do is in their own self-interest. This is especially true for newbies and nonprofessional traders. It's a weird quirk of human nature that we find unconscious ways to sabotage our own efforts, to do things that hurt rather than help us. This tendency is our financial death wish, which I call our "inner knucklehead." It's what makes us do stupid things and then wonder why we did them. You may find this whole idea hard to digest at first. You'll ask, *Why would anyone except a very troubled person* try *to fail financially? Why would anyone engage in self-sabotage in a place like the market, where everyone's looking out for themselves? Hey, Batman, riddle me this—what's the evolutionary purpose of a financial death wish?*

TRADER TALK   A *newbie* is a new, inexperienced trader.

I'll leave it to the psychology books to explain the theories. What I *can* tell you is that *the financial death wish is real, and no one in the market is immune.* I see traders fall victim to it every day. The deep motivations are probably different for everyone, and figuring out yours is a job for your therapist. The important thing is for you to recognize your inner knucklehead and prevent it from losing your money.

Common Self-Defeating Trading Behaviors

Some examples will show you what I mean. Here are some very common self-defeating behaviors that most traders think they're immune to. But if I had a dollar for every time I've seen these going on, I'd stick a coupon in each of these books entitling you to a free sushi dinner, on me!

1. The newbie's exuberant leap into the market.

During a bull market, how many thousands of people open up online brokerage accounts? How many others start buying particular kinds of stocks because they've heard they're hot? Many hundreds of thousands. Lots of these people have absolutely no experience in stock trading or investing. Many are so excited about becoming a stockholder or market player, or just raking in the ka-chingos, that they can't wait to jump in, ready or not.

It's not only new traders who leap before they look. Even experienced traders can feel a rush of irrational exuberance when they see something that *might* be too good to miss. Besides, it may seem easier and more pleasant—*at first*—to jump in and let the chips fall where they may. And that's exactly what will happen, because jumping in half-assed is a casino mentality. It's no better than gambling at the racetrack, at cards, or at a roulette table. Few would disagree that compulsive gambling is self-defeating behavior, but our society's blind faith in the stock market makes us believe that throwing money at stocks is somehow different. It isn't different. It's your inner knucklehead at work.

The way to control this species of inner knucklehead is to learn and practice the discipline and skill of trading. Think of it as a form of martial art, with its own kind of spiritual beauty. The chapters that follow will help you learn. It's your job to continue to learn every day and to use what you know to make intelligent decisions on every trade. *That's* the way to make the ka-chingos!

2. The passive investor's blind faith in Wall Street's advice.

Blindly following the investment advice of a broker or analyst is one of the most financially self-destructive things I can imagine. I should know—I did it not once but twice and, baby, I lost *big* both times! It's tempting to just put your money "in good hands"—or what you *want to believe* are good hands. You imagine that it's like putting your valuables in a safe-deposit box. After all, the market always goes up in the long term, right? And isn't buying stocks the best way to invest? Haven't lots of people gotten rich by making good investments? Isn't it the American way?

What you *have* to realize is that the market *is nothing at all* like a safe-deposit box. Neither is a stockbroker. First, there's no safety in the market. Second, a broker's interests and your interests *are not the same* and actually *are often completely opposed* because the broker gets paid a commission when you buy stock, whether it's a good investment or not. A broker's primary job is to make stock transactions. Putting blind faith in a broker is like expecting McDonald's to design a healthy nutritional plan for you. They'll recommend whatever they've got for sale, whether it's good for you or not. This is why *all brokers suck!*

Equity analysts, like the ones on TV, are even worse. They're true salespeople who are paid to talk up the stocks of companies that are their firms' clients. *All analysts suck!* And mutual fund managers are required to invest their funds' money whether it's a good time to do it or not—and collect management fees whether the funds gain or lose money. In Chapter 6 I'll tell you about the "window dressing" manipulation that fund managers engage in to make their funds look like winners every quarter.

Your inner knucklehead loves to watch you sit back and put your trust in the judgment of others. It's so much easier than educating yourself, and they're *professionals*! But it's never their money at risk, and they profit from your transactions whether you do or not.

This misplaced trust can be overcome once you decide to take charge of your own financial future and learn how to beat the Wall Street suits at their own game. There's a lot of joy in coming out miles ahead of these so-called professionals!

3. The small account holder's failure to diversify.

Another temptation your inner knucklehead will dangle before you is to put all your money into one or two stocks that you *hope* (always beware of that word!) are going to do ridiculously well. The reasoning would be: Why dilute the ka-chingos by spreading the money among too many stocks? Some investors with very little capital (under $5,000) might also be tempted to put all their eggs in one basket because trading fees significantly cut into profits on very small investments. (See Chapter 2 to find out how to assess your trading capacity realistically.)

The problem with failing to diversify is that, even though diversification may dilute the profits you make on a single stock or sector, it also softens your losses if that stock or sector crashes and burns. Putting all your money in one place is very, very risky—just the kind of thing your inner knucklehead *loves* to do, since all it can see are the huge ka-chingos if things *happen* to work out well. Your inner knucklehead lusts after the upside and ignores the downside.

Once again, the way to keep your inner knucklehead under control is with education and discipline. You'll learn a lot about both in the chapters that follow.

4. The perfectionistic day trader's refusal to accept small losses.

Some people think they're pretty good at trading, and they let this belief get in their way and make them worse traders in the process. People who want to be good at trading—and who doesn't?—sometimes think they have to be right on *every trade*. When a stock they thought would go up starts heading down instead, and it's clear that the trade is not going according to plan, they want to hold on to it until it goes back up again, and they convince themselves it will do that eventually. They don't want to lose a cent on a single trade, and in most cases this really boils down to being unable to admit that the trade didn't work out.

This makes no sense and is nothing but stubbornness. And, if you think about it, isn't it *incredibly arrogant* to think you could be right about *every trade*?

There are several reasons why holding a losing stock that keeps going down and down, losing more and more money, is financially self-defeating behavior. First, there's a real chance that the stock will *never* recover to the break-even point. Second, even if it finally does recover, holding a loser ties up your capital and makes you unable to take advantage of good trading opportunities for days, weeks, or months. You'll finally make it back to zero instead of making ka-chingos, which is the reason you're trading in the first place. Third, obstinately holding on is an example of the unfocused, planless trading and lack of discipline that eventually cause traders to lose all their money.

But wait! says your inner knucklehead. *It's stupid to take a loss right away, because the stock is bound to make a comeback as soon as you sell it—some variation of Murphy's Law will make it come back!*

Sure, this is possible. Anything is *possible*, but what matters is what's *likely*. It's *at least* as likely that the stock will go even lower before it turns around. At that point, if you had gotten out earlier and there was a good, sound reason to believe that the stock would start back up, then you'd be free to go for it—making some ka-chingos by rebuying it at the lower price.

And even when a stock does go up again right after you've sold it, you have to realize that there will be *many, many more times* when this *won't* be the case if you make a habit of clinging to bad trades. Holding on to losers is a losing strategy.

Every trader must be willing to take small losses. If you're not willing to take small losses or don't have the discipline, you shouldn't trade.

5. The emotional trader's mood swings between invincibility and panic.

Remember the story of Mr. Loser? When the price of his stock rises, he feels invincible (*I am one with the market!*) and buys more and more. When the price goes down, he panics and sells and wallows in self-hatred (*I suck!*). Instead of buying low and selling high, Mr. Loser buys high and sells low, which is a fail-safe way to *lose* money.

The emotional trader needs to understand how the market works, what to expect from it, and how to get what he or she wants from it. Then he needs to develop the skill and discipline to quiet his emotional inner knucklehead and listen to his own good judgment.

6. The distracted trader's attempts to trade on bad days.

There will be days when you just shouldn't trade. There will be days when you're simply not up to it. If you're feeling sick or upset—if you have the flu, have just experienced emotional pain or a nasty surprise, or are feeling angry at the world—*just take the day off.* If you're physically hurting, you won't trade well because you won't have the energy to concentrate and make yourself do the right thing. You won't care enough, and you'll just screw things up. And if you're emotionally hurting, you *really* won't care enough. You may be grieving, feeling guilty, or hating yourself. Unconsciously, people in those emotional states *don't want to win.* Unconsciously, they want to do things that will hurt or punish themselves.

No one has to trade every day. On a bad day, be kind to yourself. Take a walk or a nice hot bath. Leave the market for another day.

Which patterns apply to you?

These are only a few of the common mistakes that traders make and keep repeating. I'm sure some of them will sound familiar. Which ones can you relate to? What other kinds of risky, money-losing behavior have you found yourself repeating? These mistakes, and others like them, are often caused by the "seven deadly sins plus fear" I discuss in Chapter 5. Like a little red devil on your shoulder, your inner knucklehead will try to convince you to commit those trading sins. *Your inner knucklehead operates by talking you into taking unnecessary and unjustifiable risks. It convinces you that taking these risks makes sense.*

This is the time to identify the forms your own inner knucklehead likes to take. It often morphs from one form to another to try to catch you off guard. *Your job is to learn to recognize your inner knuckle-head at work.* Once you can recognize its influence, you can respect its power and control it.

I should know. It took me a while to figure out the ways I was unconsciously sabotaging my trading and to avoid making the same mistakes over and over. When I first started out I traded emotionally, always afraid to miss the boat, chasing stocks up and paying too much for them, then selling them in a panic for large losses. I repeated this cycle enough times to wipe out my entire investment. Finally, by learning to trade with a plan, with planned entry and exit points for all my trades, I began to control this losing pattern.

Once I learned how to buy and sell more intelligently, I found that my biggest weakness was failing to diversify—getting carried away with one promising stock until I'd put so much money into it that it became risky. In Chapter 5, I refer to this as the sin of Gluttony. You could also call it "going nutso on one trade." This type of bad trading cost me a fortune several times. The first time, I overloaded my account on a single stock for an IPO spinoff play that I thought would be the mother of all trend plays. What I didn't realize at the time was that the market was starting to turn sour and the trend was weakening for the time being (see Chapter 6 for more on how and why trend plays work). Though the percentage loss wasn't crushing, I had so much money tied up in that one stock that I lost all the prof-its I'd made in the preceding three months.

The second time I let Gluttony rule my trading, I was only slightly smarter. Instead of putting most of my money into one stock, I put it into a lot of stocks—in one sector. That sector, the biotechs, had been ultrahot, with many large and small issues running up from 15 percent to 40 percent a day, and sometimes even several hundred per-cent in a day when good news broke. So I had a whole stableful of those fine little racehorses—they made up over half my portfolio.

Well, after a little while the biotechs crashed in a spectacular heap of test tubes and lab coats. I had even seen that trouble was on its way, but my positions were so big that I actually couldn't sell them out fast enough to avoid huge losses. (You never thought having a huge account could be a problem, did you? See Chapter 2 for a discussion of the special problems of very large accounts.) There I was, trapped like an enormous, slow beast whose power can't save it from its fate.

Since then, I've learned to keep a close eye on my inner knucklehead's gluttonous tendencies. I've learned to *just say no* to the temptations of going whole hog on any stock, sector, or single type of play. I've learned to stay nimble and move with the market, rather than expect the market to do whatever it is I have in mind.

My other major weakness is still an emotional one: specifically, emotional bad days. But now I know that I don't need to trade every day, so when I'm upset or just not in the mood to trade, whether it's because I'm burned out on it or because I have too many other things on my mind, I just do something else. It takes *attentiveness* to recognize when you're not up to trading and *discipline* to back off on those days, but believe me, it will pay off *royally*. On the days you trade, baby, you've got to *play to win!*

Take the First Step Toward Improving Your Trading

How can you gain control of the self-defeating patterns that are holding back your trading? There are two things you can do right now.

STEP 1: *First, identify the dominant types of risky trading you've noticed in yourself.* Be brutally honest. This is about tough love, not making excuses. Write them down and rate them by importance.

STEP 2: *Second*, and most importantly, *make a commitment to understanding and working within your own limitations.* That's the way winners become winners—in trading, in sports, in politics, and everywhere else. Your inner knucklehead will always be with you. If you try to deny and avoid seeing your weaknesses, you'll have blind and vulnerable spots that will make you lose. By embracing your limitations and working within them, you'll learn how *you* can trade most effectively while avoiding the traps your inner knucklehead will *always* keep trying to lay for you.

RULES OF THE GAME   Control your inner knucklehead.

RULES OF THE GAME   On a bad day, take a walk.

RULES OF THE GAME   Play to win!

Chapter 2

Getting Real

Defining Your Trading Capacity

This chapter covers:

- How to approach online trading realistically, based on your own practical limitations
- How to assess time limitations
- How to assess capital limitations
- Why margin trading is a powerful and useful tool
- Why margin trading must be used with care, especially in uncertain market situations
- How to assess online access limitations
- How to choose an online broker that suits your needs

Keeping It Real

You've seen advertisements that try to scare people away from online brokers and back to traditional high-fee brokers (you know, the ads that came out a year or two after the ones that said online trading was the inescapable wave of the future). You've heard about people who lost all their money in manic online trading frenzies (though maybe you've heard just as much about people who made piles of money). Your friends have warned you against trading stocks online, repeating the horror stories and shaking their heads in dismay. But you know money can be made in any market, bull or bear, and you think you've got the stomach for online trading and the ability to master a new skill. Maybe you've been messing around with stocks for a while and have finally decided to get serious. Maybe you're a fairly accomplished trader who needs to overcome a few bad habits. Or maybe you're a complete newbie who's a cowboy at heart and can't resist a good challenge. Whoever you are, the point is that you've decided to give trading a closer look.

The prophets of doom are right on one point: online trading isn't for *absolutely* everybody. More importantly, though, it works for lots of people—but different kinds of people in different situations need to go about it differently. This chapter will help you identify your capacities and limitations so you can get real about how to make online trading work for you.

Getting Real About Time Limitations

Trading involves a time commitment. To do it right, you have to figure out how many hours you have to devote to the task and choose your trading style accordingly. Start to think about it by asking yourself a few questions about the time you have for activities related to trading.

The first question you have to ask yourself is this: Are you going to trade full-time, or are you going to do it part-time while holding down another job? Unless you have enough capital to make a comfortable living by trading *and* preserve your financial cushion, even when the market is sluggish (see the discussion of capital limitations below), my advice is what every beginning actor and musician hears when first starting out: *Don't quit your day job.* In other words, begin by trading part-time. Even part-time trading will require at least an hour or two a day for monitoring the market and your portfolio, as well as staying familiar with stocks you think might make good trades.

Especially if you're trading full-time, the second question you have to ask is how much time *outside* market hours you can commit to trading. Basically, there's no limit to how much time you can spend, but you don't need to make it your life. If you're trading only the morning NASDAQ gaps, you can do it in an hour a day (see Chapter 3 for an explanation of fading the gap up and gap down). If you're trading full-time, though, it'll take a bit more time than just 9:30 to 4:00. You won't be able to roll out of bed at 9:25, switch on the computer, rake in money all day, and then log off at 4:05 to bask beside the pool with umbrella drinks until midnight. Plan to put in an hour or two each day outside market hours.

But what could take so much time? you ask. There are two main things: *learning to become a good trader,* which takes long-term study and time, and *keeping up with the market*, which takes some time each day. Remember, you want to *rule* the market! While you're learning to be a better trader, you'll want to make use of all the resources you can find, digest them, and refer to them again and again. And even when you've become a pretty good trader (though the education never ends, believe me), you have to keep up with what the stock market is doing and what's going on with different sectors and individual stocks. This is called *research*, and it's *not optional*. You should constantly be aware of current market psychology and conditions, which change every day. Every market is like a living being that has experiences and reacts to them. It has moods, habits, and a personality. Understanding the market is like getting to know a person. And, like getting to know a person, it can happen only by paying close attention over a period of time.

Especially if you're just starting out, you should spend some time every evening looking at stocks and sectors, charts and news. This will help you understand why the market did what it did that day, as well as anticipate what will happen the next day and plan a strategy and some possible trades. You'll rise and shine each morning between 7:30 and 9:00 to tune in to CNBC and check the futures and overnight news, and you may follow premarket trading beginning as early as 8:00. Aftermarket trading continues until 7:00 or 8:00 P.M., depending on the ECN. (There has been talk of 24-hour trading, but that hasn't happened yet.)

The point here is that *you can't be a successful trader if you're half-assed about it!* As jazz musicians say, you gotta pay your dues—no one gets a free ride. Trading is work! But you don't need to devote all your waking hours to it. Choose your style and make sure you have the time to do it right.

Getting Real about Capital Limitations

Should you trade full-time or part-time?

Many people dream of becoming full-time traders. It's easy to see why. Trading lets you work at home—*you can even do it naked!*—and you have no boss and no office politics to worry about. There are no deadlines. You can take a day off whenever you want. There's huge potential for ka-chingos. And your success or failure depends only on you.

But, besides the other questions you should be asking yourself (such as *Will I mind spending all day in front of a computer?* and *Do I want to give up my other work?*), an absolutely crucial question is whether you can *afford* to trade stocks for a living—yet. This will depend on the answers to two other questions:

- How much do I need to make per week, on average?
- How much can I expect to make per week, on average?

If the answer to the second question is *comfortably* greater than the answer to the first question, you can probably afford to trade for a living. If it's not, you'd better wait.

You should know the answer to the first question already. The much harder question is the second one. The answer depends on a number of factors, as discussed below, but it *absolutely* depends on how much capital you have available for trading, because your potential return in real dollars is limited by the size of your account. Example: What's the average weekly dollar amount you'll make if your average weekly return is 2 percent? Well—uh—2 percent of *what*? A person pulling in 2 percent a week on an account of $100,000 will be making $2,000 a week. Someone trading $10,000 and making 2 percent a week will gross $200 a week. You get the picture.

When you're figuring out how much capital you have available for trading, realize that you *must* have some reserve—a financial cushion—if you plan to make your living trading. You need a cushion even after you've become a competent trader and are making pretty consistent returns. Your reserve should be even bigger if you're just starting out. There will be days when it doesn't make sense to trade, either because the market just stinks or because you're not in good shape, either physically or mentally. There may be long periods—even weeks at a time—when the market is so choppy or so stagnant that trading will only churn your account and eat away at your capital. So if you want to trade full-time, *you must be financially secure enough that you'll never find yourself trading scared.* If you trade afraid, you're *much* more likely to lose money.

WAXIE'S STREET SMARTS

Trading scared makes you *much* more likely to lose.

Okay, let's say you know how much you can put into your account. The tricky question is, what kind of return can you anticipate?

There's no sure answer to that question, only conservative estimates. Your return will depend on a host of factors, including your experience and skill levels, the state of the market, whether you're trading on margin, and whether you plan to take money out of your account regularly or allow it to grow (ah, the joy of compounding!). Let's take a look at each of these factors.

First, experience: if you're a complete newbie, you should be prepared to lose money at times during the first few months you trade, and on occasion after that. I *don't* mean you should *expect* to lose— *you should never expect to lose*, because that kind of losing mentality makes it seem all right to lose, and if it seems all right, you'll *let* yourself lose instead of doing what you have to do to win. (Anyway, if you really expect to lose, then why are you trading?) But you have to be prepared to pay a little for your trading education, and it'll take a while for you to develop consistency in your trading judgment.

WAXIE'S STREET SMARTS

Never *expect* to lose. Instead, learn to manage and reduce risk.

Do you see the difference between expecting to lose and protecting yourself?

Next, there's your skill level. Even experienced traders aren't equally skilled at trading, and most people are more skilled at certain styles of trading than others (see Chapter 3 on how to find your own trading style). After all, how many things is everyone equally good at doing? Not many—that's just the way life is.

On the other hand, no one should *ever* think they're stuck at some predetermined or genetically based skill level. *No way!* Everyone, from best to worst, can improve their trading by learning and practicing. Your skill level will depend on the effort you've put into developing yourself as a trader, how well you follow the rules of the game, your temperament, and your enthusiasm for trading. As my friend and technical-analysis guru Tiny says, *Luck = hard work + discipline + opportunity.*

Another major factor affecting your return is the state of the market. During the bull market insanity of a few years ago, average weekly returns of 20 percent to 30 percent—or even more—were quite possible. This may happen again from time to time in certain sectors, but it isn't something to count on. In more subdued market climates, rallies may bring 2 percent to 15 percent returns but won't happen as often or last as long. When the market is trending downward and you're primarily selling short, your returns will be more limited than in a bull market. This is because you can't do more than double your money on a short sale and, at least with some brokers, you can't increase the size of your positions by buying on margin. (If you don't know why, see Chapter 10 on shorting.) And when the market is seesawing up and down without establishing any definite direction, it can be hard to make money consistently at all. On choppy days like that, you should seriously consider sitting on your hands and preserving your capital—knowing when to stay out is a very important part of the game.

All these estimated returns assume that you've got your trading game together and aren't making lots of costly mistakes. Even assuming all that, you should realize that you'll occasionally have a week that ends in a net loss, though you should do all you can to avoid it. Remember that this is a marathon, not a sprint. The key to success is to keep at it, making profits slowly and steadily.

RULES OF THE GAME   It's a marathon, not a sprint.

What can we expect of the market in the future? Obviously, the future is impossible to predict—and anyone who says he or she can predict it long-term is just messing with you. *For traders, the long-term direction of the market really doesn't matter* because traders can make money in any market. We should simply assume that the market's direction will vary a lot: There will be isolated weeks when it will be possible to make 20 percent or more, weeks when you'll make 1 percent to 5 percent, and weeks when you can hardly trade at all because the market lacks direction. If you expect change to be a constant in the market, you'll be nimble and ready to switch direction quickly. You'll be able to go with the flow of the market, and that's the hallmark of good trading.

Besides market conditions, another important variable in your potential return is whether or not you're trading on margin.

Margin, used properly, is an incredibly useful tool that can increase your percentage return by 100 percent or more. What is this magic tool? Buying on margin means using the shares you hold in your account as collateral to borrow money from your broker to buy more shares. If you've set up a margin account, most brokers will let you borrow an amount equal to at least the total value of the stocks you hold, and possibly more, depending on your trading history and the size of your account.

T R A D E R   T A L K   *Buying on margin* means using the shares you hold long as collateral to borrow money to buy more stock.

What does this mean? Well, let's say your account is worth $20,000. If you buy stock worth $20,000, you'll have available margin of $20,000, and with it you can, in theory, buy an additional $20,000 worth of stock. That means if you made a profit of 8 percent on your account *without* using margin, *with* margin you'd make 8 percent on *twice* as much stock—which is the same as making 16 percent on your actual capital. *Ka-chingo!* Of course, the flip side is true as well: If you lost 8 percent of your account's value without using margin, you'd lose twice as much if you were fully margined: 16 percent of your account's value. *Just shoot me now!* This is why margin is a double-edged sword and why *you must have the proper respect for your margin capacity*. Another important rule is to buy long on margin only during periods when the market is solidly trending upward. Margin buying is very risky in uncertain or fast-changing market situations.

There are a lot of other important things to understand about margin trading which are outside the scope of this chapter. See Chapter 11 for more on how to use margin effectively and keep yourself out of trouble.

T R A D E R   T A L K   A *margin call* is a call from your broker saying that your losses have made you exceed your margin capacity and that you must deposit enough money into your account to bring you back within your borrowing limits; otherwise, the broker will sell enough of your holdings (at the current very low price) to raise the cash to meet your margin requirement. If the market is falling very quickly, the broker may not even call you—it can just liquidate your positions and let you know what happened afterward.

N E W B I E   T R A P   Going hog wild with margin is a recipe for disaster. Margin calls are *way* beyond bad news. If your broker sells your positions, you'll have unspeakable losses and will be left with little, and maybe no, capital remaining for a comeback. It's entirely possible to lose your entire account in a margin call. You could even end up owing the broker money.

Used carefully, margin is a wonderful tool, but you have to understand what you're doing and avoid taking foolish risks.

The last thing your potential return depends on is whether you'll be taking money out of your account on a regular basis or allowing your trading capacity to grow with your profits. Letting your account grow is similar to compounding in an interest-bearing account. For example, if you started with $50,000 and made 8 percent the first week ($4,000), the following week you'd have $54,000 to trade with; if you made 8 percent again the second week (now $4,320), you'd have $58,320 to trade with the third week; if you made 8 percent again the third week (now $4,665.60), you'd have $62,985.60 to trade with the fourth week; and so on. By contrast, if you took all the profits out of the account while making 8 percent a week on $50,000, you'd make $4,000 every week and your account and dollar return wouldn't increase at all. Either of these approaches is perfectly fine; they just mean different potential returns.

So, back to the big question: what's a reasonable estimate of your average weekly return if you're trading full time? The honest truth is that I'd only be making things up if I tried to guess what someone, anyone, could expect to make per week or per year. Remember that any estimate you make is of an *average* weekly return, since your *actual* return will vary a lot from week to week. Assuming that you're somewhat experienced and trading well but not perfectly, using margin at least occasionally, periodically taking money out of your account, and trading in an up-and-down market that regularly goes through untradable periods, it's certainly possible to double your money or better in a year if you're trading full-time. Of course, nothing is guaranteed; this is just a reasonable estimate of what's possible. On the other hand, one trader I know took an account of $1,500 and turned it into $150,000 in six weeks during the spring of 2001. I turned less than $50,000 into millions in a little over a year. It's hard to give you a more specific answer than that. The best idea is to make a *conservative* estimate of your returns and let yourself be pleasantly surprised if they turn out to be better, rather than expecting too much and then making less than you need to live on.

Should you trade at all?

Maybe your plan is to start trading with a very small amount of money at first, just to see how it goes, and use more later. Or maybe you can spare only a few thousand dollars to fund your account. If your starting balance is small, there's another aspect of capital limitations you need to think about: the extra challenges people face when they trade with small accounts.

Small means less than $5,000. Even accounts of between $5,000 and $10,000 are harder to trade than larger accounts, but it gets progressively easier as the account gets bigger (at least until your account is really a monster).

Before listing the challenges of trading small accounts, I should add that they have some advantages. For one, it's much easier to enter and exit positions quickly when they're small than when they're huge. When you're trying to get rid of thousands of high-priced shares (or tens of thousands of cheapies), there simply may not be enough buyers to purchase them all. It may take a long time to sell them, and you may be vulnerable to major losses if the price is falling and you're unable to exit the position. A trader holding a small position rarely encounters this problem. The mouse can usually escape from the thicket that traps the elephant.

Besides making you more nimble, trading small positions makes your actions almost invisible. Trades of less than one hundred shares don't even show up on Level I quotation systems, while big trades send signals to the market and can even move prices, often to the disadvantage of the large-position trader. Traders buying or selling large positions often have to enter positions in stages to avoid making their intentions obvious.

Now for the challenges in trading small accounts. One disadvantage is that it may not be possible to use margin. Some brokers, for example, won't let you trade on margin if your account is worth less than $2,000. This not only means that you can't borrow money to buy extra shares, it also creates a bigger problem: *If you don't have margin capacity, you can't sell short.* This means you'll be sidelined much of the time during down-trending markets. These problems will disappear, though, once your account's value tops $2,000, or whatever your broker's margin requirement happens to be.

Another problem with accounts of less than $10,000 is that most direct-access brokers (see below) require a minimum account balance of $10,000. If you don't qualify for a direct-access account, you'll have to trade with a slow, unreliable Web-based e-broker and will constantly be at a disadvantage until your account has grown enough to qualify for a direct-access account.

A new problem has arisen with the amendment to NASD Rule 2520, which restricts rapid trading in accounts containing less than $25,000. Check with your broker to see how many times you can buy and sell a single stock in the same day during a five-business-day period. If your account contains less than $25,000, options trading may be a useful alternative.

Besides the limitations brokers and the government impose on small accounts, there are also some more fundamental challenges. First, there's the important issue of trading fees. For small accounts, the cost of making a trade is always large relative to the size of the position. If you place a trade worth $2,000 and your broker charges you around $20 for a limit order, the fee has lost you 1 percent of your capital before the stock even does anything. Exiting the position will cost you another 1 percent. In Chapter 9 I state the rule that you should never lose more than 2 percent of your portfolio's value on any one trade. This rule has to bend if you have a very small account, and that means increased risk.

A small account also makes it much harder to diversify your portfolio. Diversification is as important in trading as it is in investing. In general, it doesn't make sense to put less than $3,000 or $4,000 into any stock position you trade. This means that if your account is worth $8,000, you'll find yourself holding only two stocks at a time. And that means you'll be risking half the value of your portfolio on each of them—which is not ideal money management. A related problem is that having enough capital for only two or three stocks at a time really limits your flexibility: You'll quickly get fully positioned and have no reserve in case a great trade comes along later.

Finally, having a small account can feed the desire to make buckets of money at warp speed, which can lead a trader to take excessive risks such as overusing margin or trying to hit home runs with riskier plays instead of consistently hitting singles with solid plays.

TRADER TALK   A *single* is a respectable return on one trade, such as 3 percent, 5 percent, or 8 percent. *Ka-chingo!*

A *home run* is an incredible return on one trade, such as 40 percent, 75 percent, or 100 percent. *Wowsa!*

If you want to start off small but can spare more than a few thousand dollars to fund your account, it makes sense to bring it up to at least $5,000 so as to avoid the worst difficulties of a very small balance. If you can't spare more, that's okay—just be aware of the challenges and make allowance for them when you judge whether a trade is safe and likely to succeed.

Getting Real about Access Limitations

To trade online, you have to have reliable online access. Obvious, no? But access constraints can arise from lots of sources you may not have thought about, including you.

The first thing to do is assess, realistically, how much time every day you'll actually be able to track and trade stocks at your computer—as opposed to sitting in three-hour-long office meetings in conference rooms, getting projects done under deadline pressure, or attending to other duties. Figure out whether there are certain times of the day when you'll consistently be able to trade and monitor positions. If you have regular online access at certain times during the trading day, you may be able to build a trading strategy around those constraints. For example, if you have access before and during the opening hours of the market—say, between 8:30 and 10:30 A.M. Eastern time—plus a fast Internet connection and a direct-access broker (see below), you can trade the gaps up and down every morning (see Chapter 3). This strategy works especially well for people living in the Pacific or Mountain time zones, since they can trade from home for an hour or two every day before going to work. As another example, if you work fewer than five weekdays each week, you can trade on your days off. There are lots of possibilities; see what kinds of creative solutions you can come up with.

The point here is to be realistic about how much *attention* you can commit to the market. Trading demands a certain amount of time and attention every day you trade—at least two or three hours, on average, while the market's open as well as another hour or two when the market's closed. Read and think about the questions in the Exercises section at the end of this chapter. Weigh your priorities, make a plan, try it for a week or two, and see if it works.

Another major access issue is the quality of your equipment— your computer and Internet service provider. Do you have a slow computer and dial-up Internet service that you get through an out-dated modem? Or do you have a fast, high-capacity, state-of-the-art computer with a broadband connection to the Internet such as cable modem, ISDN, DSL, or T1? The quality of your Web access and hardware will make a *huge* difference in your trading.

If you're serious about trading, I recommend the following: A relatively new computer with as much memory as you can stuff into it and a hard drive capable of running sophisticated trading software; two or three monitors (one for your trading and portfolio-tracking software, one for a Level II quote screen, and possibly a third for communications with other traders and Web research on company news, market updates, and such; if you don't have a third screen, you can do communications and research on one of the other screens); and a printer for printing out your list of positions, occasional order screens and execution reports, and any other information you'll want on paper. Your Internet connection should be *at least* as fast as a 56K modem, and preferably a broadband connection. What you want is something ultrareliable that isn't going to periodically flake out on you by cutting you off or slowing down. Those things aren't just annoyances; they can really cost you the big bucks, and that's excruciating.

If you have a medium-sized to large account (over $10,000) and are serious about trading, you should have access to Level II quotes. Level II is available by subscription for a monthly fee, but some brokers provide it to higher-volume traders free of charge. You should also have access to real-time charts, which are available from proprietary charting software companies such as Quote.com and from various direct-access brokers such as TradePortal.com.

TRADER TALK   *Level II* is a real-time streaming stock quotation system that shows all market makers' and electronic communications networks' posted bid and ask prices and order sizes. It therefore shows whether there is selling or buying pressure and how great it is, as well as lots of other useful information.

By contrast, *Level I* is a basic stock quotation system that shows only the *current best* bid and ask prices and order sizes, along with the price and size of the last executed trade and its percentage change from the previous day's closing price. Real-time Level I quotes are available for free on most Web-based online brokers' Web sites as well as on sites such as TrendFund.com, FreeRealTime.com, and RagingBull.com. These brokers and sites also provide information such as the stock's opening price, high and low of the day, and current volume.

Be nice to yourself and get a comfortable office chair, too. You'll be at your desk every day for most of the trading day, and you don't want to develop aches and pains as a result of your trading. Go ahead and get cozy—trading should be fun!

The last thing you'll need is a good broker.

Getting Real About Brokers

Your trading capacity will depend on the kind and quality of the broker you're using. The faster and more dependable your broker is, the better your trading will be. If your broker constantly causes delays and irregularities, your profitability will suffer, and trading will become annoying instead of fun.

There are three kinds of brokers: old-fashioned live brokers (*they walk! they talk!*) whom you have to call on the phone; Web-based online brokers; and direct-access online brokers. To trade successfully, you need a fast, reliable *online* broker. Waiting for somebody to answer the phone and do your trading for you definitely won't cut it. The markets move way too fast for *that* kind of bulldinky.

So, then, what's the difference between the two types of online brokers?

There's a *big* difference. With Web-based brokers, like DLJ Direct, Fidelity, Schwab, Datek, and E*Trade, placing an order essentially means sending an e-mail to the broker, who forwards it to a market maker such as Knight Trading Group, who actually executes the trade. This has a couple of important implications. First, there are greater time lags while all these communications take place, and the additional steps mean more opportunities for delays and screwups to occur. Second, the broker doesn't actually execute the trades; the market maker does. Although the market maker is supposed to get you the best available price, the actual execution price is completely out of your and the broker's control and often *isn't* the best. Market makers are in the business of making money, too, and if they can get an extra .05 per share out of a trade instead of giving it to you, they will. (Of course they're not supposed to, but the world isn't a perfect place, as you should know by now.) Third, a Web-based broker doesn't give you access to all the Electronic Communications Networks, one or more of which may offer a better price at any given moment than a market maker.

T R A D E R   T A L K   A *market maker (MM)* is a firm authorized to buy and sell securities on an exchange at publicly quoted bid and ask prices.

T R A D E R   T A L K   An *electronic communications network (ECN)* is a computerized exchange system that makes market makers' and other parties' orders available for execution by third parties.

On top of that, most Web-based brokers have fee or other payment arrangements with particular market makers based on the size of order flows. For this reason, these brokers may preferentially route your orders to their preferred market makers even if another MM is offering a better price. A Web-based broker may also have an ownership interest in one of the ECNs, and may preferentially send it orders for that reason. This biased order routing can cost you a lot of money over time.

By contrast, direct-access brokers, such as TradePortal (which I use) or CyberTrader, give you direct access to the electronic systems the market makers use as well as to all the ECNs and the stock and options exchanges themselves. This eliminates the extra step of routing through a Web-based broker. Instead, the direct-access broker's system electronically searches for the best available price among all the market makers and ECNs as well as the exchanges themselves, and has your order executed at that price. All this usually occurs within a fraction of a second. A direct-access broker that has no preferential routing arrangements and automatically seeks and finds the best price in the market is going to save you a *bundle* of money in the long run. The speed of direct access to the market will save you a bunch, too, since delays in fast-moving markets can be extremely costly and can prevent you from making certain types of trades at all (for example, playing the morning gaps up and down).

Direct-access brokers generally have their own trading software for you to install on your computer. If you want to use a direct-access broker at home but are planning to do part of your trading from work, you should find out whether you can trade from your office computer. If you can't install the trading software at your office because of computer network arrangements or firewalls, find out whether you can reach your account through the Web.

Other things to consider when choosing an online broker are fee arrangements and the availability of options trading. If your account size is moderate to large, minor differences in the size of fees per trade are probably not as important as the overall quality of the broker, but you should make sure your broker's fees are competitive with those of other brokers of its type. Some direct-access brokers charge a monthly fee for the use of their software in addition to per-transaction trading fees, but most provide discounts or free software use if your trading volume is high enough.

Far more important than fees is the availability of options trading. Being able to trade options is an incredibly useful tool, because it can be highly profitable and because you can use options as a hedge against the risk in your stock trades. Although a full discussion of options is outside the scope of this book, I *highly* recommend that you set up your trading account with both options and margin capabilities instead of opening a plain-vanilla cash account. That way, those capabilities will be available when you're ready to use them.

Finally, find out whether your potential broker's customer-service department is helpful and available. You'll experience an occasional screwup with any broker, and believe me, being able to avoid the headache of slow or unresponsive customer service is worth its weight in gold.

Now take a look at the questions below. They'll help you get real about your trading capacity, and understanding that capacity plus the stylistic factors you'll identify in Chapter 3 will help you create your own personal trading style.

Exercises

I. Should you trade full-time or part-time?

- Are you a complete newbie?
- Do you have enough capital to comfortably make enough to live on *and* preserve an adequate financial cushion if you trade full-time, allowing for the ups and downs of your own learning process and for periodically sluggish markets? (see question III below)
- Do you *want* to be a full-time trader, or do you have other work that you don't want to give up?
- Do you mind sitting in front of a computer screen all day?

II. What are your time limitations?

- Can you spend several hours each day during market hours monitoring your trades, the market, and promising sectors and stocks?
- Can you spend several hours each evening doing research and learning to be a better trader?

III. What are your capital limitations?

- How much money do you need to make per week, on average?
- How much capital will you start with?

- Is your financial cushion adequate?

- How experienced a trader are you?

- Will you use margin for trading?

- Will you regularly take money out of your account or will you let the account grow?

- As a conservative estimate, how much can you expect to make per week on average?

IV. What are your online access limitations?

- Can you count on having computer access during the times you're planning to trade?

- Do you have the flexibility to keep an eye on the market and your positions while performing your duties at work?

- Can you avoid being so distracted by other work concerns that you can't exercise sound trading judgment?

- Is your schedule predictable, or are you often called away from your desk?

- Are your equipment and Internet connection up to the task of trading?

- Is your online broker fast, reliable, and unbiased in its order-routing practices?

- Does your online trading account include margin and options capabilities?

V. What are your dreams?

- Think hard about this question, and keep thinking about it in the coming days.

- What are your financial dreams?

- What are your other lifetime dreams?

Chapter 3

....

I Just Gotta Be Me

....

Finding Your Own Trading Style

· ·
This chapters covers:

- Why different personalities require different trading styles
- The benefits of a flexible, active trading style
- Different active trading approaches:
  - Day trading
  - Trend trading
  - Fading the gap
  - Trading based on technical analysis
  - Options trading
- How to learn trading skills
- Why trading must differ from gambling
- How to develop a winning attitude
- How to make trading fun

If You're 6'5", You Can't Be a Jockey

Every trader has his or her own style. How could it be otherwise?

Everyone's personality is different, and everyone has a unique combination of strengths and limitations. Even people who excel at the same things don't excel in the same way. Look at top athletes. Even within the same sport, some excel through superior strength, others through strategic thinking, and still others through sheer physical grace. They use their greatest talents to make up for other areas where they aren't quite as strong.

Likewise, some of us are slow, others fast; some have a high tolerance for risk, while others want to feel secure. None of these traits is better than another; they just give us some limits to work within. And let's face it—if we could do everything, we'd become so confused by our limitless choices that we'd never really be able to accomplish anything.

For example, when I was a kid, I loved to watch horses run. What if I had developed a life's ambition to become a jockey? What if I'd decided that riding the winner to the finish was the only career for me?

That career choice would have created a big problem, because I was not a small kid. In fact, I was the opposite of small. By junior high, I was so tall that it would have been crystal clear that I had a snowball's chance in hell of becoming a jockey. I kept growing and growing, eventually ending up at six-foot-five.

It would have taken me a while to accept the fact that I had a limitation that prevented me from doing something I wanted to do. But gradually I'd have learned to work with what I'd been given. As it was, I took up baseball, became a good pitcher, and have found lots of advantages in being a big guy.

Some people are cut out to be hypercaffeinated day-trading dynamos who make hundred of trades a day to capture tiny price movements. This isn't my style, and I personally don't think it's the best or most profitable one—the commissions alone can kill you. Most people have no desire to make hundreds of trades a day, and most wouldn't be any good at it anyway.

The point here is that we all have different personal styles—it's just a matter of finding out what works for you.

How do you find your own trading style?

The way I found mine was the same way I've learned everything about trading: through trial and error. I don't think there's any other way to do it. You can read a hundred books (not a bad idea, anyway), but until you put what you've learned into practice, you won't be able to see what makes you money and what doesn't. As you read about the different trading styles below, don't overanalyze them and try to predict what will work for you. It's pretty hard to know until you've taken them for a few test drives.

Some traders stick to pretty much one single style, and others use two or more or really mix it up with many approaches. My style is an active one that's mostly based on trends, but it's flexible because I'm also willing to use any other available trading tool that makes me money. There's no one approach that works all the time, and different things work at different times if you know how to use them.

Active Trading Styles for Your Toolbox

These are some of the active trading styles and techniques I have in my toolbox and use often:

- Day trading
- Trend trading
- Fading the gap up or gap down at market open
- Technical analysis
- Options trading

The more you understand all the trading techniques available for you to use, the more you'll have to choose from, and the more flexible and intelligent a trader you'll become.

What's involved in each of these trading techniques, and what does each require of traders? First I'll explain what they all have in common, and then I'll describe their differences.

It's All About the Momo

TRADER TALK *Momentum ("momo")* is the strength (due to volume) of the buying or selling that's causing a stock's price to move. When a price movement has momentum behind it, the movement is more likely to continue in the same direction, at least in the short term.

TRADER TALK A stock's *volatility* is the degree to which its price moves up and down. A highly volatile stock experiences large price fluctuations, while a more stable stock does not. A particular stock's volatility can vary over time according to market and stock-specific conditions.

Trading is not about the fundamental value of the company, and it has little to do with the company's true future prospects. In other words, it's got almost nothing in common with investing. Instead, trading is about capitalizing on price movements that can be dramatic—*the crowd goes wild!*—but don't much matter in the long term. *All trading is about momentum—the big momo.*

When a stock has momentum, it's like a ball that's been given a push: It's going to roll for a while before it stops. How fast and how far the ball rolls, though, depends on many other things, like the surface it's on (rough or smooth, inclined or flat), opposing forces (such as wind), and what kind of ball it is (fully inflated, soft, irregularly shaped, and so forth). When a stock is showing some momentum because lots of people are starting to buy it, you have to figure out the state of the market it's moving in, whether there are opposing forces (upcoming resistance levels or flocks of short sellers ready to pounce because of the company's bad long-term prospects), and what kind of stock it is (what sector, how strong a company, size of float).

TRADER TALK A stock's *float* is the number of issued shares available for public trading. Because momentum depends on supply and demand, the size of a stock's float can affect its potential for volatility.

Stocks with relatively few outstanding shares can fairly easily encounter situations where demand far exceeds supply, thus creating a lot of momentum. For example, when a stock with only 8 million shares outstanding suddenly becomes popular, it can zoom up in price much faster than a stock with 800 million shares outstanding.

What creates momentum in a stock? Let's think about upward momentum—rapidly increasing price with increased volume—and its basis in market psychology and basic economics. When lots more people want to buy the stock than want to sell it, the increased demand will be greater than the available supply. When demand overtakes supply, the price goes up because sellers realize they can ask for much more and get it as buyers compete with each other for shares. It's a seller's market. The price rises higher and higher until something happens to make it stop—the price reaches a level where no more buyers are willing to pay the price, sellers think it's not going to get any better and they'd better clean up while they have the chance, or new information appears about the stock that makes its value decrease.

The same concept holds for downward momentum—rapidly decreasing price, also with increased volume—but in this case more people want to sell the stock than buy it. It's like rats leaving a sinking ship—except that the leaving is what's making the ship sink. There's way too big a supply, nobody wants to buy, and sellers start lowering the price to get rid of shares. It's like an overstock sale—it's a buyer's market. The price falls until the price reaches a level that's so low no more sellers are willing to sell out, buyers think it's a bargain that's not going to get any better and is too good to pass up, or new information becomes available that increases the stock's perceived value.

Increased demand to buy or sell also usually means increased volume: When there are more shares changing hands because of increased buying or selling, the volume (total number of shares traded) increases. And these two things—changing price and increased volume—have another effect, as well: They draw attention to the stock. When something is moving more than it usually does, people want to know why. They'll take a look at it and try to figure out the reason. If they can find a reason, they may decide it's a reason for them to buy or sell, too. If they can't find a reason, they may decide it's only a matter of time until the reason becomes obvious, and that once that happens, the price may move even more; in this case, they buy or sell because they want to be in or out of the stock at a good price when the news finally comes out.

TRADER TALK *Volume (trading volume)* means the number of shares of stock traded in a particular period of time. Volumes are tracked for individual stocks and also for entire stock exchanges.

Momentum can build and continue over minutes, hours, days, or weeks. The time frame of the momo a trader looks for determines that trader's style. Let's look at some examples.

Day trading

TRADER TALK Although the term's been used loosely to describe a lot of active trading styles, true *day trading* is hyperactive stock trading in which a trader can make hundreds of trades each day, attempting with each trade to capture extremely small price movements such as 0.1 to 0.3 dollars per share on stocks that are making momentum moves. A day trader often holds positions between a few minutes and a few hours. Most day traders routinely end the day "flat"–holding no stock positions, only cash.

TRADER TALK A *scalp* is a quick trade, lasting a few minutes, for a small profit.

True day traders live and die by intraday volatility. They look for little spurts of momo and try to jump in and out of stocks as they rise (or fall, if they're shorting) to catch a little slice of the action—to get a scalp. And they do this many, many times a day—even hundreds of times. Day traders usually trade with a very large amount of capital—they have to, to make trading for such small percentage returns worthwhile. They figure that if they can capture little price movements enough times, at the end of the day all their scalps will add up to a worthwhile profit.

This can be a useful tool at times, and sometimes a trade that you thought would be longer-term turns into a scalp when you've got a small profit and realize you want out because the situation has changed. That's fine. As a primary strategy, though, I don't believe that pure day trading is a good way to make money over the long term. Few people succeed at it. The problem is that intraday volatility is so short-lived and changes direction so fast that you end up losing almost as much money as you make, and your trading commissions add up to be staggering. Also, each trade involves risking a huge amount of capital for an extremely small percentage return—a typical scalp could be worth as little as 0.1 percent and usually won't be higher than 2 percent. This is a *very* high risk-to-benefit ratio. On top of everything else, pure day trading is really stressful. You need to have hair-trigger reflexes, and you have to be glued to the computer screen every minute you're trading. To me, that's not fun, and trading should be fun.

That's just me, though. The pure day-trading style is perfectly suited to some people's abilities and personalities, and I sincerely wish them the best. I also hope they stay at it, since by constantly buying and selling huge lots, they create volatility that I can trade on in other ways!

Trend trading: Trends are your friends!

TRADER TALK   *Trend trading* is a style of trading in which a trader identifies market trends, or patterns, that occur again and again. By knowing when a stock is likely to exhibit trend behavior, the trader can anticipate price movements and capitalize on them.

T R A D E R T A L K   *Swing trading* is a strategy that involves holding positions for fairly short periods of time, such as a day to a week, to profit from
short-term price movements. Swing trading is really a subtype of trend
trading that deals mainly with short-term trends but is much slower-paced
than day trading.

My style is based primarily on trend trading.

Where a day trader tries to scalp fractions of dollars on ultrashort
trades, usually for percentage returns ranging from 0.1 percent to
2 percent, the idea of trend trading is to net much bigger profits—
5 percent to as much as 50 percent, or even more during a strong bull
market—by holding the stock from hours to days or weeks.

Trend trading is a much more laid-back style than day trading (but
then, what isn't?). What trend trading requires is a lot of thought,
planning, and attention to trends—recurring patterns—in the market. A trend is a pattern that's repeated again and again in the market
and can be relied on to reasonably anticipate the price movements of
stocks in similar situations.

T R A D E R T A L K   A *trend* is a pattern that is repeated by different stocks
and can be relied on to reasonably anticipate the price movements of similar stocks.

There are hundreds of different trends in the market. For example,
one of the strongest trends is the earnings trend: Quarter after quarter, stocks with upcoming earnings announcements that are expected
to be favorable begin, about two weeks prior to the scheduled
announcement, to gradually rise in price. Other examples of recurring medium- to long-term trends are price runups before stock
splits, price decreases after stock splits, runups before earnings
announcements, runups before IPO spinoffs, price decreases immediately after IPO spinoffs, runups in stocks that are about to be added
to major stock indexes, price decreases before IPO lockup expira-

tions, and runups due to "window dressing." (See Chapter 6 for a full discussion of different types of trends and how to look for them.)

I find trends in the market that occur over and over again, then use them to anticipate price movements in specific stocks and take positions in those stocks before the movements happen. Trends occur in both bear and bull markets. They won't always be the same trends, because trends only last for a certain amount of time before they become well-known and lose strength (in this way they're like fads: Once enough people have their Razor scooters, the mystique wears off, it's not cool anymore, and the fad fades away), and because different trends are seen in bull markets and bear markets. Still, the stock market can never go for long without developing new habits and patterns that start to recur, and trading on a new trend will be just as profitable as trading on the old ones. That's why trends are your friends!

Most of my money has been made playing trends.

RULES OF THE GAME   Trends are your friends.

Fading the gap at market open

TRADER TALK   A *gap up* is an opening stock price that is significantly higher than the previous day's closing price. For the entire market, a gap up is when the market opens higher than it closed the previous day.

TRADER TALK   A *gap down* is an opening stock price that is significantly lower than the previous day's closing price. For the entire market, a gap down is when the market opens lower than it closed the previous day.

NASDAQ stocks often open at prices significantly higher or lower than their prices at market close the day before. A higher open is a *gap up*, and a lower open is a *gap down*. The open is followed by a period of volatility that lasts for around half an hour. During this volatility, the price usually moves a bit more in the same direction as the gap (upward after a gap up, downward after a gap down) and then reverses to close the gap—to return to near the previous day's closing price. (It's very rare, though not impossible, for a stock to gap up and then just keep on going up, or for it to gap down and continue to go down without a bounce.) On a gap-up day, the reversal downward to close the gap often ends in what will turn out to be the low of the day, and on a gap-down day, the reversal upward often ends in what will turn out to be the low of the day. The morning gap is a trend, but it's a particularly predictable and resilient one. To some extent, it's the result of a structural phenomenon, something built into the way the NASDAQ works.

What makes NASDAQ stocks gap up and down in the morning?

There are two facts responsible for the pattern of gaps followed by volatility. The first fact is premarket trading between 8:00 A.M. Eastern and the market's open at 9:30 A.M. (during the premarket, only institutions and traders with premarket access can trade, and their activity can make the price of a stock rise or fall considerably). The second fact is that anyone with an online trading account can place overnight orders between the time the market closes (at 4:00 P.M. Eastern) and its reopening the next day. They can, and many do.

These overnight orders aren't executed during the premarket. They all wait in a big pile for the market to open at nine-thirty. The market makers, whose job it is to fill them, can see whether there are more buy or sell orders. And a lot of the people who place overnight orders—the naive and foolish ones—place market orders instead of limit orders. (*Never, ever* place an overnight market order! *This is one of the most brain-dead things you can do!*) So when the regular market finally opens, that big, helpless pile of orders is lined up to be executed first thing. And the traders who placed them should be executed, too, and put out of their misery!

WAXIE'S STREET SMARTS

*Never, ever, **ever** place an overnight market order!* It's the same as saying, *Steal my money!* Placing overnight market orders is one of the most foolish things a trader can do.

The whole situation plays out pretty predictably. Let's say there are a lot more buy orders than sell orders. The market makers have every incentive to drive up the price in the premarket, so the stock opens with a gap up to begin with. Then the rush of pent-up demand drives the price up even more, and it's driven up all the faster because of all those market orders just screaming to the sellers and market makers, *Take advantage of me! Charge as much as you want, because there's no limit to what I'll pay for this stock!* Besides the backed-up overnight orders, some clueless traders and investors inevitably see the price rising after the market opens and decide they need to jump in, too, driving the price up even further.

In the same way, if there are a lot more sell than buy orders, there's a gap down and pent-up selling pressure drives the price down further, again all the faster because of the overnight market orders and by people who panic and sell when they see the price going down after market open.

Back to the gap up example: As market makers fill all those defenseless market buy orders, the price of the stock runs up until there aren't any more orders left to fill; then, as soon as the buyers dry up, the price drops back down to some level either near the opening price or even below it, closing the gap, and everyone who bought on the way up sees their stock lose value immediately.

This happens almost every day.

So, how does the smart trader play the gaps up and down?

What works most days there's a gap is to *buy the gap down* or *sell or sell short (or sell and then sell short) the gap up*. This technique is known as *fading the gap* because, by trading against it, traders make the price gap close or fade. Fading the gap means buying near the lowest point in the volatility after a gap down, with the expectation that the stock price will bounce right back up after all the sellers have been shaken out. Likewise, when there's a gap up, you'll sell short (or sell a stock you've been holding overnight) near the highest point in the volatility after the gap up, anticipating that the price will zing down again after all the backed-up buy orders have been filled.

Lots of traders do this every morning there's a tradable gap, and it's all some traders do. West Coasters can do it every day before they go to work. I fade the gap just about every day there is one, including gaps on stocks I'm holding long for other trend plays, which I sell on the gap up and later rebuy using the 10 A.M. rule to reestablish my positions. (The 10 A.M. rule is explained in Chapter 8.) If I'm short, I buy to cover on a gap up and reshort later.

Fading the gap has made me tons of extra money, and it's good trading to take a profit that's offered to you on a gap. In fact, I'd say it's bad trading not to. This technique is quite fast-paced, though, so if you don't have a direct-access broker and Level II quotes, it may not work well for you. Web-based brokers' sites can be very slow during the first half hour or so of the trading day, especially during periods of high trading volume.

Technical analysis

TRADER TALK   Trading based on **technical analysis (TA)** relies on the study of price and volume charts and other market data to discover trends and significant price levels (**technical indicators**) that reveal probable future stock-price movements.

Just about any trading style relies to some degree on technical analysis, or TA, and every trader should know at least the TA basics. Technical analysis is a big part of research: By looking at historical price charts, you can see where a stock's been, for how long, how it got there, and where it seems to be headed. Without this knowledge, you'd be flying blind.

Technical analysis is mainly about charts. There are also market indicators such as the Trading Index (TRIN) that tend to indicate whether the market is bullish or bearish. There's a lot to learn about charting: how to find support and resistance (see Chapter 9); how to use trend lines and momentum indicators; how to tell if the market is overbought or oversold; candlesticks; and lots of patterns and configurations. Why isn't analysis of charts just a lot of hocus-pocus, like reading tea leaves? It's because lots of other people, including professional traders working for five-hundred-pound-gorilla enterprises like banks, mutual funds, and other institutional investors, are looking at the same charts, seeing the same patterns, and acting on them. The fact that a price of 27.0 is a resistance point for ARFF doesn't mean that 27 is the most a share in the company can possibly be worth, based on a true and absolute valuation of the company performed by the magic of the market; it just means that that's a price the stock couldn't overcome before, so now everyone will have their eyes on 27 to see if ARFF can break through the level this time. For that reason, everyone will become cautious in their buying of ARFF as the price approaches 27.

In other words, there's a lot of self-fulfilling prophecy in TA, but that's the way the market works. It's not about the *real* value of the company—no one really knows what that is. Instead, it's all about how the game is played.

As I see it, there are two possible ways to handle TA. The first is to read books on the subject, such as *Technical Analysis of Stock Trends* by Robert D. Edwards and John F. McGee and *Beyond Candlesticks* by Steve Nison, and become a competent or even an expert chartist. It will definitely help your trading. (It would be a mistake to think TA is the be-all and end-all, though, because *lots* of other factors, such as news and nontechnical trends, come into stock and market behavior.)

The other is to use teamwork: to find a trading buddy who is very good at TA and have that person handle the sophisticated chart analysis while you keep on top of news and nontechnical trends or perform some other useful service. I found a trading buddy, Tiny (don't let the name fool you!), who's a very talented technical analyst, and working together has turned out extremely well for both of us.

Except for the explanations of chart-based information you'll find in later chapters, a full discussion of technical analysis would require an entire book of its own. Make learning the basics of technical analysis part of your trading education. It will really open your eyes.

Options trading

T R A D E R   T A L K   An *option* is a contract that gives the owner the right to buy or sell a specified amount of a stock or other security (for a stock, generally 100 shares) at a specified price until a specific *expiration date*. A *call* is an option to buy, and a *put* is an option to sell. On its expiration date, an option becomes worthless unless it's been exercised.

T R A D E R   T A L K   A *naked call* is a call position in which the person writing the call doesn't own the number of shares of the underlying stock the call would require if exercised, or hasn't deposited the amount of cash equal to the call's exercise value.

A *naked put* is a put position in which the person writing the put doesn't have a short position in the underlying stock of the size the put would require if exercised, and hasn't deposited the amount of cash equal to the put's exercise value.

....
WAXIE'S STREET SMARTS

Options are tradable securities. You don't have to own shares in a stock to buy its options; instead of writing options contracts, just trade them. You can buy and sell them at a profit before the expiration date without having to exercise them.

Although options trading is a somewhat complicated topic all its own and can't be covered in a book like this, it's another extremely useful tool that I use all the time. One of its most important uses is to hedge risk. For example, if you hold a stock position that's somewhat on the risky side, you may want to take an opposing position with options. Let's say you're holding Dream Big Software (RUNT) long for earnings. RUNT is expected to have good earnings, but the market has been sour and unsteady and could do a major tank job if there's any bad economic news. You decide to hedge your risk by buying some puts on RUNT, which will make money if RUNT's price goes down. This way, if RUNT goes up, you can sell the stock for a profit, and if RUNT goes down, you can sell the puts for a profit.

Don't try trading options until you've educated yourself about how they're priced and how they work. There are some important complexities to options. For example, if you don't sell your options by their expiration date, they can expire worthless and you can lose all the money you put into them. Also, you have to be able to figure out the risk-to-reward ratio on your whole hedging strategy and to have a plan to exit both the stock and the options positions so that they don't cancel each other out.

You can also buy options instead of stock, or in addition to stock, when you see a great trend-trading opportunity. While options are riskier than stocks, their potential reward is huge relative to that of stocks. A successful options play can bring in 50 percent, 100 percent or even more. Basically, the risk and potential reward on options are both much greater than on stocks. The best approach is to become a competent stock trader and then learn to trade options as a next step.

Some traders' style is to trade only options. This is, uh, an option, but you'll probably prefer to trade a lot of stocks, if possible, because stocks generally have more liquidity and are easier to trade, and also because some stocks don't have options available. I think options are best used as a supplement to stock trading.

Learn about options. They won't always be the answer, since they can be risky, but they can be enormously profitable when you need a hedge or see a solid trend-based opportunity.

These five trading styles are only a few of the choices you have to draw on. There are lots of others. For example, some traders trade many stocks, while others trade only one or two stocks, getting to know them so well that they can make good money by trading the same stock every day. I knew a trader who traded Exxon Mobil Corp. every day for years and made a living doing it. Some traders concentrate on large, high-volume stocks, while others focus on stocks of any size in whatever is the week's hottest sector. Think of all these styles and ideas as useful tools, try them out, and see which ones work best for you. To help you think about some of the issues that may affect your style, take a look at Exercise I at the end of this chapter.

Your First Steps As a Trader

If you are new to online trading, the first steps you take in finding your style and learning to trade must be safe ones.

Before you start to trade with real money, you need to spend some time following stocks and learning to understand patterns, trends, and the quirks of individual stocks. The best way to do this is by trading on paper or in a simulated account on the Internet. This will help you gain experience and develop your trading style—and make beginners' mistakes—without losing your capital.

Paper trading basically involves writing down in detail all the trades you would make, including the number of shares, entry price, and entry time. Be scrupulously honest about what you do and when—it does you no good to pretend that you really would have bought the stock five minutes earlier at a better price when in reality you wouldn't have, or to leave a bad trade out when you calculate your account performance.

Even more realistic than paper trading is managing a simulated online account. For example, at **www.trendfund.com**, you can place virtual online stock trades and keep track of your performance almost like you would with a real online account. A site called **www.investorfactory.com** also offers a good online simulation game. Simulated accounts are great because they give you the opportunity to make exactly the same mistakes you'd make trading a real account online, and there's no way you can fudge your performance to make yourself feel better. If you do well with your simulated account and start to feel bad that you weren't using real money and making real profits during that time, *stop* feeling bad. If you're really doing what you should, you'll continue to do well when you start to trade with real money. The market isn't going to go away. There will always be other stocks to trade. And it was just as likely that you would have made a horrendous blunder and lost half the money in your account—if this had happened, think of how glad you'd have been to lose only cybermoney!

Some basic resources to use as you start to learn about the markets are as follows:

- **www.trendfund.com:** free real-time Level I quotes, trader education, current company and economic news, market updates and summaries—and, of course, Waxie!

- **www.freerealtime.com:** free real-time Level I quotes and portfolio tracker

- **www.yahoo.com (Yahoo! Finance):** detailed company and stock information, such as float and short interest

- **www.ragingbull.com:** free real-time Level I quotes

- **www.quote.com:** free real-time Level I quotes and streaming real-time daily charts

- **www.cbsmarketwatch.com:** search engine to find news by stock ticker symbol

Exercise II at the end of this chapter will help you start to recognize market trends by monitoring and analyzing two stocks' behavior over a week's time.

The Market Is Not a Casino

While every successful trader's style is unique, there is one style you won't see in any of them: a gambling mentality.

Some people honestly think that trading, especially day trading, is gambling, and that for traders, the market is just a glorified online casino. *Whoa there, cowboy!* For *successful* traders, this could not be further from the truth.

Any business or financial venture involves fluctuation and risk. Everything from investing to something as down-home as buying the local ice-cream parlor involves financial risk—any time you put money into a venture, you could end up losing some or all of it. This has been true since the dawn of capitalism. The whole idea behind any legitimate business venture is to *manage risk responsibly*. More often than not, good money management is what separates winning from losing traders. (See Chapter 11 for a full discussion of money management.)

Gambling is not a legitimate business venture. If you have the money to lose, it's recreation, and if you don't, it's either desperation or addiction. There's no risk management involved; you just throw in your money and wait to see what happens, and what happens doesn't depend on anything you do. It's random chance.

Any trading approach that's essentially gambling or is based on a gambling mentality can't succeed. Honestly, a lot of people who call themselves investors are really involved in long-term gambling—as little as they know about the companies they invest in, and as unlikely as a ridiculously overpriced market is to keep going up for another five years, what else can you call it? If you believe that trading or investing is gambling, or if you're simply planning to throw money at stocks without a well-thought-out strategy based on market behavior, *you might as well just give your money to charity right now*, because that way at least you'll be giving it to someone who needs it. Trading involves planning, study, strategy, and limiting risk so that your risk-to-reward ratio is favorable *on every trade*. When the ratio isn't good enough, you don't make the trade.

Starting Out with a Winning Attitude

I've heard people say that you have to expect to lose money while you're learning to trade. *Not!* You should never, ever *expect* to lose money. *Expecting to lose is a loser's attitude*. It makes it seem like it's okay to lose. Instead, you should realize that trading is a percentage undertaking—not every trade will be a winner, but when a trade doesn't work out, you should never lose big because you've limited your risk and taken the right steps to kept your capital safe (see Chapter 11 on money management). If you make more on your good trades than you lose on your bad trades, you'll come out a winner.

It's important to develop a winning attitude right from your first trade. Part of getting off to a good start is to be realistic, because if you have unrealistic expectations, you'll feel like you're losing even if you're doing fine, and you'll wind up taking unnecessary risks in an attempt to do the impossible—and, if you do extremely well on one trade, you'll think all your trades have to be as good.

There are three Rules of the Game you always need to keep in mind to remain a winner. These three rules apply to any trading style or combination of styles:

1. *It's a marathon, not a sprint.* Trading is not a get-rich-overnight scheme. It's a way to make money by working at trading over a long period of time. You don't want to burn up your capital in your first weeks by trying to make a million the first month. Think about marathon runners: They know they have to run for 26.2

miles, so they'd be idiots to start out at breakneck speed. If they did, they'd be burned out after the first five miles. Instead, they find a steady pace they know they can keep up for several hours, and in this way they make the distance. The same is true of trading. Your outlook has to be long-term. Otherwise, you're going to make bad mistakes. If you feel like you have to double your money by next week, you probably shouldn't be trading.

RULES OF THE GAME   It's a marathon, not a sprint.

2. *No one makes money every day.* No real trader in the history of the markets has made money every day. If anyone tells you they do, they're lying! It's just not the way trading works, and there's no reason it has to. Thinking you have to make money every day is like thinking you have to win on every trade—it's insane, and it will make you do desperate, foolish things to try to meet unrealistic expectations. *You don't need to make money every day.* If you trade well, you'll make lots of solid trades and occasional monster profits—and over time, your account will grow into a beautiful thing.

RULES OF THE GAME   No one makes money every day.

3. *Swing for singles, not home runs.* The key to good trading is to plan solid trades that have a good probability of doing well—a good risk-to-reward ratio. If they work well enough to keep you profitable, you're doing exactly what you should be doing. If they sometimes exceed your expectations, that's a bonus. Professional baseball players don't try to hit home runs every time they're at bat. They know that most of the time it's much smarter to go for a safe hit that will get them to first base and advance other runners, rather than try for a homer and risk hitting a fly ball that will be caught and put them out. That's exactly what it's like in trading. Always aim for a solid but modest return, and gratefully take more when it comes to you. Just because you *aim* for singles

doesn't mean you have to limit yourself to small gains if the stock goes wild; it's just a matter of controlling your expectations. If you hold on to a trade too long, trying to force it to return more than it's safe to expect, you'll take on too much risk and end up worse off than if you'd just cashed out with a modest profit. Anyway, four modest profits of, say, 5 percent, 3 percent, 4 percent, and 8 percent will add up to the same return as one trade returning 20 percent—even more if you're allowing your account to compound—and are probably much safer plays.

RULES OF THE GAME   Swing for singles, not the fences–and often you'll hit home runs anyway.

Keep Your Trading Fun!

Whatever your trading style turns out to be, there's one thing that's got to be part of it, and that's *having a good time*. Trading can mean sitting by yourself with a computer for many hours a day, so you need to be creative and not let yourself stay too serious all the time.

Amuse yourself. Talk back to the market and to CNBC, and tell them what's what. Do a happy dance when a trade goes well. Do an ecstatic dance when it's fantastic. Chat online with other traders, joke around, and spread the knowledge and the love.

My morning ritual helps me keep it fun. When I trade, I go into battle as a lean, mean street-fighting ninja. First I put on my black socks and black underwear. Black is the color of the ninja. Then I swallow my green juice, a concoction of thirty-nine greens mixed with water. It's got a mean smell and a wicked taste, and it gives me strength for the day's battle. Two large glasses of carrot-beet juice stand at the ready. It may be magenta, but it's the fuel the ninja needs. Now I'm ready for battle. *Bring it on!*

RULES OF THE GAME   Make trading fun.

Exercises

I. Comfort level with quick entries and exits and short holding periods

Think about the following questions:

a. Can you make snap decisions comfortably?

b. When you make snap decisions, are they good ones?

c. Can you change your mind quickly if a decision starts to look like a bad one, or do you get stubborn about being right?

d. When you change your mind, can you act on your new strategy quickly?

e. Do you have a fast Internet connection?

f. Do you have a trading account with a high-quality direct-access broker?

g. Does the idea of holding stocks for only a few minutes and doing this fifty to over a hundred times a day seem fun and challenging, or would it drive you crazy?

h. Do you enjoy video games?

i. Does the idea of holding stocks for only a day, a few days, or a week seem appealing, or would it make you feel insane?

j. Does the idea of holding stocks for a few days to a few weeks, and occasionally longer, seem enticing, or would it drive you mad?

II. Stock monitoring for newbies

An important part of trading is getting to know the market and stocks intimately. The approach that works best is to get to know one area very well instead of trying to learn everything about every type of market. For example, you may wish to concentrate only on NASDAQ stocks, and only on those in sectors related to computer technology and biotechnology. These stocks have been volatile in recent years, and volatility generally makes for good trading. If you're aware of other hot sectors, they may be worth getting to know.

To become more familiar with the market, do the following exercise. Choose two NASDAQ stocks in different sectors. (Computer technology and Internet sectors include semiconductor manufacturers, wireless-technology companies, broadband-delivery companies, Internet service providers, Internet portals, fiber-optic networking companies, software manufacturers, and Internet incubators; biotechnology sectors include genetic-engineering companies, genetic-information providers, and stem-cell technology companies.) Make sure that one has a large float (over 500 million) and the other has a small float (under 20 million). Find out what the two companies are in the business of doing, in ten words or less. Identify the other stocks in their sectors.

Look at historical data on both stocks to see their all-time high and low prices, and look at their one-month, three-month, and one-year charts. Where have they been, and where do they seem to be going? Has their volume recently become heavier or lighter, or has it stayed the same? Is the volume pattern in keeping with volume trends in the NASDAQ as a whole?

Now, every day for a week, track both stocks carefully and see how they behave from day to day. If you have Level II, find the "ax" (see Chapter 4) and watch what it's up to. Look at real-time one-minute charts each day, and look at five-day charts to see how the stock's behavior today compares with its behavior during the past few days. Check for company news. How does each stock react to company news? To news about other companies in its sector? To general economic news or Federal Reserve actions? How closely does it follow the general direction of the NASDAQ? How does it behave compared with other stocks in its sector? Keep detailed notes on the stock's behavior. What is the stock's typical daily volume? Is it five thousand, five hundred thousand, or five million? If there's a big surge in price or volume, can you find the cause?

At the end of the week, you should start to develop a feel for two things: how a single stock behaves and how one stock's behavior differs from another's. When you start to trade, you'll want to be closely attuned to the behavior of stocks so that you can decide when a change is significant and when it's just a hiccup that doesn't mean anything important.

Part II

The Mind Game

Chapter 4

....

Meeting the Enemy

....

Learning to Think Like "Them"

•••••••••••••••••••••••••••••••••

This chapter covers:

■ How market behavior reflects human nature

■ Who your market opponents are

■ How knowing your opponents will improve your trading strategy

■ How market psychology drives trends

■ General types of market trends

■ How changing market conditions affect your strategy

The Market Runs on Psychological Energy

What is the market thinking?

To some traders, the market seems as mysterious and unpredictable as the weather would without meteorologists and satellite photos. One day it's up, the next day it's down; stocks go up and up for months even though everyone says they should have stopped weeks ago, and finally they tank one day a year later for what seems like no particular reason. Right when everyone says the market will never stop going up, it dies; after days of carnage, market analysts say it's at its bottom, but it goes down further; people stop calling the bottom, the carnage gets worse, and then people suddenly start buying again. Stocks make zigzag lines on charts; if they're worth $60 a share, why don't they just go up to $60 and stay there? Why do stocks in good companies lose money for months and then one day recover? Isn't the market efficient? Doesn't it reflect companies' true values?

It's time to change the way you think about the market. It's time to stop thinking about it as some kind of godlike machine in capital letters—*The Market says this, The Market says that*—and understand it for what it is. The market is a game with a bunch of players who are all out for themselves with the single goal of trying to take money away from each other, and they're all following the most basic and familiar rules of human nature and psychology. These players aren't equally powerful, though, and they all have different functions, interests, and limitations. These differences make them behave in different ways. You're one of the players, too, though you're a very small one.

The more you trade, the more you'll see how the behavior of the market and its players starts to fall into familiar patterns. So does the price behavior of individual stocks. Why is this? Aren't we told that the short-term price behavior of stocks is random?

The behavior of stocks and markets is* not *random. The reason patterns develop is that the market is made up of people, and everything that happens in the market is a result of their actions. People are creatures of habit, and they're also fairly rational—when they find something that works, they tend to repeat it until it doesn't work anymore. Then they go looking for another strategy to rely on. But remember that people are only *fairly* rational—their irrational and emotional side lets them give in to exaggerated expectations, either bullish or bearish. Their tendency to act on these expectations causes market swings, which create moneymaking opportunities for you.

Once you become familiar with all the players in this game—with your opponents (your enemies, if you think of trading as warfare like I do)—the market will make a hundred times more sense. Everything that happens in the market is a result of the actions of market players, and it can all be understood in terms of their motivations. Once you understand what's going on, you can analyze market moves and start to anticipate market behavior on the basis of human nature.

Market Movements Are Based on Perceptions

One of my all-time favorite movies is *Rashomon* by Akira Kurosawa, a great Japanese filmmaker of the 1950s through the 1990s. The film is about perceptions—how the same event is viewed and experienced by four people in four different ways.

Thinking about *Rashomon* gives us a clue to how you, as a trader, should view events in the market. *Your goal is not to figure out the truth.* (Is DUNG really worth 6.50? Will the market ever realize that PHAT is the greatest company of the decade and give it the valuation it deserves? When will the overpriced sectors get to their proper price levels?) Your goal is not to see *your* opinion or perception turn out to be right. What you think doesn't matter if more players in the market think differently. Instead, the goal is to figure out *what everyone else's perception is*, not caring whether that perception is right or wrong. *The market's perception right now*—"trader reality"—is what a trader cares about. If it's moving the market, it doesn't matter whether it's right or wrong—the important thing is that *it's what the market thinks*.

Part of understanding everyone else's perception of reality is knowing who everyone else is. That's why you have to get to know your enemies.

Know Your Enemies

Who are your market enemies?

Your enemies fall into four basic categories:

■ **stock analysts:** persons employed by brokerages, banks, investment funds, and financial advisors to study companies and make buy and sell recommendations about stocks; analysts are highly visible and audible in the media

- **market makers (MMs):** firms authorized to buy and sell securities on an exchange at publicly quoted bid and ask prices

- **institutional investors:** entities with very large amounts of money to invest, like banks, mutual funds, pension plans, endowments, and insurance companies

- **individual momentum traders:** day traders who are trading large accounts and moving into and out of large positions quickly, sometimes acting together in groups

In addition to these enemies, there are other players involved in the market who aren't exactly opponents but do have some effect on market dynamics. These include amateur individual investors and unskilled day traders who may act against their own best interests. The actions of these plain folk, like those of more sophisticated players, are understandable when analyzed in terms of human nature.

What are the motivations and characteristic behaviors of these large and small players?

Stock analysts

It seems like stock analysts are everywhere, and the most well-known ones (like Abby Joseph Cohen and Henry Blodgett) are practically household names. Many others appear every day on television networks such as CNBC to give their opinions about where the market is headed and their recommendations about which stocks to buy.

My opinion on this group could not be clearer: *All analysts suck!*

Why do all analysts suck? There are two reasons, both of which are important to keep in mind. First, *analysts are paid employees of brokerages, banks, and other financial institutions that have their own financial interests*. These firms are interested not only in getting investors to buy stocks (because of the commissions this will generate), but also in getting investors to buy *certain* stocks. This may be because a bank is a stock's underwriter, meaning that the company issuing the stock is a bank client who expects the bank to promote the stock; or because the firm or one of its big clients has too much of the stock and wants to unload it on the public at an inflated price; or for some other self-interested reason. The point is that analysts' recommendations are not unbiased. Second, *analysts who appear on television are expected to have opinions and say something about them even if they haven't a single solitary clue what's going on,* especially about the state of the market and where the market is headed. They're expected to come up with several minutes' worth of interesting comments for the viewers even if it's entirely groundless speculation.

The stock recommendations put out by analysts are usually just laughable. They set absurd price targets for stocks that will never reach them; they set price targets that have already been reached; and sometimes they issue recommendations that are complete and utter weasel doodie. Here's one of my all-time favorites, a report of a real recommendation that was issued near the beginning of 2001:

> QCOM coverage reiterated by SA at Strong Buy, lowered price target from $200 to $110 believing shares to be expensive at current levels in light of only moderate 2001 earnings growth.

What's wrong with this picture? Well, how can anyone seriously recommend a stock as a *strong buy* when they believe it's *overpriced* ("expensive at current levels") and *don't expect it to do anything spectacular in the entire coming year?* What kind of nonsense is that? Of course, the real question is, how high an opinion must this analyst have of the investing public to issue a recommendation that could be swallowed only by morons?

Analysts suck because they intentionally mislead people, manipulate stock prices by creating unrealistic expectations, and make market predictions without having any idea what they're talking about.

All analysts suck!

Market makers

Market makers are brokerages or banks that buy and sell stocks to fill orders from clients or other customers. Some big MMs are Goldman Sachs, Merrill Lynch, Morgan Stanley Dean Witter, First Boston, Hambrecht Quist, UBS PaineWebber, and Lehman Brothers. Some market makers have huge institutional clients that buy and sell stocks in quantities big enough to move the market. NASDAQ market makers use their own capital to keep up inventories in stocks so that they can sell to customers who want to buy and buy from customers who want to sell. Basically, they're financial retailers.

For all the stocks in which they're active, market makers must publicly quote both bid and ask prices. MMs have to be ready and willing to sell shares to customers who want to buy, and to buy shares from customers who want to sell. This means they're on both sides of every stock they deal in. But at any given time, an MM will be much more interested in one side than the other, depending on the kinds and sizes of orders they're receiving from clients. These order streams show them the direction of demand for the stock as well as how strong that demand is. A market maker will be more interested in buying than selling if it has more customer buy orders than sell orders coming in, and more interested in selling than buying if it's being hit with lots of sell orders. This is because, as customer orders come in and are filled by the market maker, it has to keep up its own inventory of shares to sell while avoiding a massive overstock.

Market makers set the prices of the stocks they deal in—they decide the price at which they're willing to buy or sell. This allows them to play games with their publicly visible prices. For example, if an MM is receiving honking boatloads of buy orders from its clients, you might think it would raise its bid and put in a large order so that it could buy the shares it needs, right away, to keep up its inventory. In reality, an MM is unlikely to do that because it would send a signal to the entire market that there's buying pressure, and that would drive the price up and create a disadvantage for the MM. Instead, the MM will try to hide its actions by putting in only a small order that it will automatically renew itself each time it's filled, or will try to bluff by actually lowering its bid. Market makers can also hide their intentions by routing their orders anonymously through ECNs.

Really? you ask. But isn't the market maker supposed to facilitate the market and act in an up-front way so the market will be transparent and efficient?

Time to get real! How do MMs make money? Besides earning client commissions, market makers make money by buying shares in the market at lower prices than those at which they sell them to their customers or back to the market. That means they want to buy shares from you for cheap but sell to you at a premium. Another way to say this is that they profit from the *spread* between their bid and their ask.

And always remember who you're *really* dealing with when you face a market maker. It's not "the bank" or "Goldman Sachs." It's not some faceless computer program. It's a person, *a trader like you,* a Wall Street professional whose job it is to make money for the firm. It's a sophisticated trader matching wits with you while acting under the pressure of having to keep up an inventory. And that sophisticated trader knows all the tricks.

TRADER TALK   The *spread* is the difference between the bid price and the ask price.

Watching the Ax Swing

The most important market maker trading a particular stock is known as the *ax*. The ax is the MM that dominates the action in that stock and tends to create price movements. This could be because the firm sells a lot of the stock in its retail business, because it was an underwriter for the company's IPO, or because its research analysts put out frequent reports on the company.

T R A D E R T A L K The *ax* is the market maker that dominates the action in a particular stock and tends to create price movements, usually because it has a particular interest in the company.

If you have Level II quotes, you can identify the ax and watch its activity. If you don't have Level II, just be aware that not every price movement you see means what you might think.

Here's an example: You have Level I, and for a few days you've been watching Rastarrific Corp. (OJAH), the Caribbean digital media giant, because of an upcoming trend play. The stock came out as an IPO about twenty days ago, and its quiet period will end soon. This means that, assuming this is a period when the trend is working, the stock's price should start to rise during the last few days of the quiet period. (See Chapter 6 for more on specific trend plays such as the quiet period play.) This morning the price of OJAH was way down, and the entire market's been sluggish and low-volume. OJAH's volume is almost nonexistent—hardly anybody's buying or selling the stock at all.

You've picked up a small number of shares at a low price, planning to pick up more later if the price goes down further or when the volume picks up, indicating that the stock is starting to move according to the trend. After you buy your shares, you notice something strange. The bid price on OJAH keeps going down, but the ask price doesn't. Instead, the spread keeps widening. This means that buyers are willing to pay less and less for shares, but sellers aren't demanding any less from someone who wants to buy their shares. The prices of the few trades that are being made keep going down. This is because those few executions are sales going through at the progressively decreasing bid prices.

In price terms, this is what you've seen: You bought OJAH when the bid was 12.5 and the ask was 12.6, so you paid 12.6. After that, the ask went up to 12.8. Someone sold at 12.5, and the bid went down to 12.3. Then someone sold at 12.3, and the bid went down to 12.1. Then the bid went down to 11.85 all by itself. Meanwhile, the ask has stayed the same— at 12.8. Now there is a sale at 11.85, and the bid moves down to 11.76.

What's up with that? The spread is over a dollar—that's more than 8 percent! If OJAH is worth less and less, why don't sellers become willing to sell for less? Has everyone been dipping into the ganja?

The answer becomes crystal clear when you think like a market maker. If you were the trader sitting at the underwriter's computer screen and trying to make some bucks for your boss, what would you be trying to accomplish, and how would you do it?

The market maker's trader knows that the quiet period will end soon. Being a professional, this trader knows all about the quiet-period-expiration trend and how it means people will soon start to buy the stock in much greater volume. And what's one of the jobs of a market maker? It keeps up an inventory of stock, because it has to be willing and ready to buy and sell to the market. The smart inventory keeper—like any profitable store—stocks up on inventory when it anticipates increasing demand, and it stocks up at the lowest possible price. If you're a trader for the market maker, then, your goal will be to stock up on shares that you anticipate are going to become a hot item in the next few days. And you want to do it for cheap, so that you can make as much money as possible on the shares when you sell them to buyers later on. Since you, the MM, can set the bid price (because no one else is buying today), you just go right ahead and do it.

On top of that, as a general rule, you'll take advantage of every opportunity you get to make a buck on a trade in any way you can. That includes making the stock sell for lower and lower prices, since at some point the low price will start triggering shareholders' stop-loss orders and making them stop out and sell their shares—to you, the market maker, for cheap! And this low-volume day gives you a perfect opportunity to move the bid and ask around so that you can accomplish two things: stock up on shares if you need them, and get shares at bargain prices that you can sell for more. Meanwhile, the ask price (which is high relative to the bid) discourages anyone from buying your shares, and this is exactly what you want because you aren't interested in selling yet.

Now that you've thought it through from the point of view of the market maker, the falling bid makes sense. The MM is trying to accumulate shares because it foresees increased demand, and it's trying to buy them at low prices from sellers who either are alarmed by the falling price or just want out of the position for reasons of their own—or from people whose stops the falling price has knocked out. And it seems to be working.

But it won't work on you, even though you bought shares at 12.6, since you can think like a market maker and recognize a fakeout for what it is. You realize that the biggest clue to this nonsense is that a big price movement is occurring *on no volume,* which means current market demand is *not* what's moving the price.

But now you notice that the ask on OJAH has started to go up, and the bid is starting to follow it up as well. Meanwhile, the market as a whole is starting to go up and take on volume. But there's still no volume to speak of on OJAH. In spite of that, the ask price increases by quite a bit with each trade, and the price just keeps rising. The ask goes from 12.8 to 12.95 to 13.0, then to 13.2, 13.4, and 13.5. *Now* what's going on? If the market maker wanted to accumulate shares, why is it selling shares and raising the price?

Once again, think like a market maker! Here you are, the MM's trader, sitting at your computer on a day when OJAH, the stock you're in charge of, is just puttering around doing nothing. You've taken the bid price way down, knocked out as many stops as you could, and bought up as many shares as possible. That game has just about played itself out. Now the market's picking up steam, and you don't want to get completely bored with this sleepy stock, so maybe it would be fun to give the impression that the stock is starting to run up and see if you can make some nice bucks on it. After all, you've picked up a bunch of shares in the low 12s and under, so if you can sell them in the high 12s or even above 13, you'll be making a whopping dollar a share. As for the inventory, you're pretty sure you'll have another chance to stock up, since the artificial price move you're creating is bound to collapse. Another possibility is that the reason your firm is this interested in OJAH is that it was the underwriter for the IPO. If that's the case, you may have more shares of this thing on hand than you really want anyway.

So the market maker gradually starts to move up the ask price. This attracts some buyers, who may have been waiting to see just how low the stock would go and now realize that it's not going any lower today. The fact that there's some buying leads to some more buying, and the price just keeps going up. Some people may think the quiet period run is actually beginning. Others just see a moving stock and think if they jump in soon enough, it will take them up a few tenths of a point. There are lots of people in the market who simply don't know what they're doing. Whatever the case, the MM's trader is now *raking* in the bucks because she's bought shares so low and is now able to sell them so high.

Now you know how a market maker thinks. If you, as an individual trader, are smart, you may want to take the opportunity to do exactly what the MM is doing and sell the shares you bought low as the ask price passes 13. This all depends on whether you think you'll get another chance to buy them back at a favorable price. If you can ride the MM's artificial price move up and sell the shares you bought for 12.6 at 13.4 or so, you'll have a nice 6 percent gain. Once many others like you start to do this, or once the buyers dry up, the high price will collapse and the stock will probably end the day right around the place it started.

Basically, market makers try to buy your shares for cheap and sell shares to you at a premium. They have the power to move prices, and at times to create artificial price movements or hide intentions that would cause real price movements. While you're learning to trade, always bear this in mind when you're trying to figure out what's going on. When you get Level II, figure out which market maker is the ax for a given stock and learn as much as you can about its characteristic behavior.

Institutional investors

By and large, rich institutional investors are the driving force behind the direction of the market. This is because they create much of the demand that drives market makers to lean toward buying or selling.

Institutional investors have buckets of money to invest. They also have staffs of financial professionals whose job it is to make investment decisions. Institutional investors that aren't mutual funds may invest their own money or may hire money-management companies to manage large amounts of money for them. Trades are often placed by these companies or through large market makers, especially a stock's ax.

Because institutions invest big piles of money, their stock orders can create large price movements. However, the fact that they buy and sell such large positions also makes them far less nimble than individual traders. That means they can create short-term price movements and trends but can't do much to capitalize on them.

For these reasons, the primary interest of an institutional investor is to purchase large numbers of shares in companies it likes at the lowest possible price within a range it believes makes the shares a good investment. In order to get the prices it wants, the institution must keep its intentions secret from the market. If its plans become known, sellers will hold on to their shares in anticipation of higher prices and buyers will start to move the stock up for the same reason. Therefore, the primary motivation of an institutional investor is to have its trades executed as close to invisibly as possible.

Sometimes it can do this by buying shares from another firm in a private transaction. If it must turn to the larger market, though, there are still some ways of buying and selling without alerting the market. One is to have a market maker purchase shares anonymously through an ECN by entering an order for a portion of the shares that keeps refreshing itself after it has been filled, for as many times as necessary to fill the entire order. For example, if the institution wants to buy twenty thousand shares of HEAT at 52, it may have its market maker enter a refreshable bid for one thousand shares at 52. When those thousand shares are bought, the quote for a thousand shares at the same price is automatically reentered so the MM can buy a second thousand. The MM will refresh the original quote nineteen times to fill the order for twenty thousand shares.

How will this look to you? There may be times when you see a stock running up like a mad thing and then hitting a level it just can't get past. For instance, you may see PHAT move from 100 to 105 to 110 in only fifteen minutes, pull back to 107.5, and then continue its run to 110.5, 111, 112, and 112.4. After pulling back to 111.6, it starts up again, but once it hits 112.0 it just stays there. It doesn't drop back down again, but seems stuck at an ask of 112.0 for a lot of 500. Meanwhile, the number of shares traded keeps going up and the "last trade" price stays at 112, so you know people are buying the shares offered at 112.

From this, you can tell that a market maker, on behalf of itself or a large institution, is selling a big lot at 112. It may have been wanting to get out of the position and finally hit its target price, it may believe the stock won't go up any further, or it may have some other reason for selling at 112. It's your job to figure out the most likely explanation and what will happen next, based on everything else you know. But there should be no mystery about the trading activity that's making the price stay at 112.

Individual momentum traders

Successful professional day traders like me live for momentum. When they see the momo building in a stock or see the makings of a momentum move, they pile into the stock and increase its momentum even more.

Momentum traders get their clues by watching orders line up on Level II, comparing the price levels and order sizes on the bid and ask sides, and paying close attention to the actions of market makers, especially the ax. They try to hitch a ride when the market maker's actions create a rush of momentum, and they may even try to play some of the MMs' own games to create false impressions of market direction.

You can see the power of day traders best in quick runups of small or obscure stocks in which institutional investors have little interest. When a stock is clearly being driven by day traders piling in and creating momentum, you have to think like a trader to anticipate what the stock will do next. Know what they look for (momentum opportunities and technical and psychological support and resistance) and understand their trading style. Then you can ride the momo with them and make some nice ka-chingos.

Amateur individual investors and unskilled day traders

There are lots of people in the market who have very little idea what they're doing. Some of them haven't the first clue. They are committing the trading sins discussed in Chapter 5, and they're trading emotionally and without a good understanding of what the market and the other market players are doing or why. When you're looking for an explanation for a market move, don't forget to consider this group.

What Exactly Is "The Market"?

Okay, so there are all these different players who have different levels of power, knowledge, and expertise. When the NASDAQ or another index moves, who is driving it?

It's a combination of all these players, of course, but when the market makes *really* big moves, institutional investors drive them because institutions have the most money. When a correction occurs, it's because institutions are pulling their money out of the market. Sustained marketwide rallies are spurred by institutional buying.

What's "the market" for an individual stock? In general, you should focus on whoever has the ability to move the stock's price and is likely to do so. Trends are formed by the interaction of all the market players, but certain stocks are affected by one group more than others. For example, large, prominent stocks are generally moved by institutional investors, while momentum in obscure stocks is usually created by day traders.

How Market Psychology Drives Market Trends and Dynamics

Market trends are driven by the collective psychology of the players in the market. This mass psychology creates many recurring patterns and other market dynamics, such as the following:

- Psychological resistance levels
- Common intraday price and volume movements
- Price movements based on stock-specific developments
- Price runups in speculative stocks
- Hot and cold sectors and sector rotation cycles
- Differences between objective common sense and "trader reality"
- Price movements based on technicals
- Contrarian indicators

Each of these trends and market dynamics makes sense when viewed in terms of market psychology.

Psychological resistance levels

The market is made up of people, and people are creatures of habit. When a stock that was at 5.00 goes on a mad run upward and breaks through all its historical resistance levels, where will it stop? If it gets past 8, I'll put in a limit sell order at 9.95. Why? Because 10 is a *psychological resistance level*. Traders watching the stock go past 8 will say things like *I think I'll sell once it gets to 10* and *I wonder if it'll continue past 10*. They don't say *I'll sell once it gets to 9.2* or *I wonder if it'll break through 11*. People tend to think in terms of round numbers, like the next integer on a two-dollar stock (in other words, 3) or the next multiple of five or ten on a more expensive stock. Likewise, if a stock has already gone up 17 percent for the day, I wouldn't be surprised to see it travel the rest of the way to a 20 percent gain, at least momentarily, but I'd be much more skeptical of its blowing past 20 percent. And if it managed to continue to 23 percent, I'd be selling as it approached 25 percent. Even if it ended up continuing to a 50 percent gain for the day, it might first pull back from 25 percent, allowing me to rebuy if I wanted. People treat certain numbers as milestones. If there's no historical resistance level because the stock is in blue-sky territory, assume that traders will create their own psychological resistance levels at round-integer price levels and round-percentage-gain levels.

TRADER TALK   A stock makes a **blue-sky breakout** when it's broken through its last historical resistance level—the last technical ceiling that could stop its upward progress.

Common intraday price and volume movements

In the last chapter, we discussed the reasons for the NASDAQ's typical morning gap up or down followed by volatility: a combination of superior knowledge and power on the part of market makers (the knowledge of whether the piled-up overnight orders waiting to be executed at market open are mostly buy or mostly sell, coupled with the ability to run the price up or down in the premarket) and unsophisticated traders' and investors' placement of overnight market orders. The morning gap and volatility pattern is just one common intraday price and volume trend seen in NASDAQ stocks.

Another is the lunchtime slump in volume and price. Between roughly the hours of 1:00 and 2:30 Eastern, traders go off to eat lunch, and the volume in most stocks falls off considerably. A stock price that's found a fairly stable level or established a definite direction by late morning often sags a little during this period.

Like many trends, this one is self-fulfilling: Because traders know that many other traders are less active during lunchtime, they

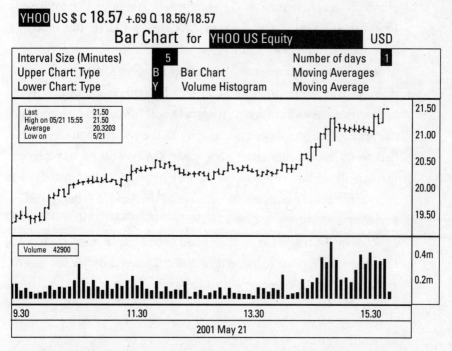

YHOO US $ C 18.57 +.69 Q 18.56/18.57

Bar Chart for YHOO US Equity   USD

Interval Size (Minutes)	5		Number of days	1
Upper Chart: Type	B	Bar Chart	Moving Averages	
Lower Chart: Type	Y	Volume Histogram	Moving Average	

Last 21.50
High on 05/21 15:55 21.50
Average 20.3203
Low on 5/21

21.50
21.00
20.50
20.00
19.50

Volume 42900

0.4m
0.2m

9.30   11.30   13.30   15.30

2001 May 21

become less active, too, reinforcing the trend. For this reason, the lunchtime slump can be a good time to pick up stocks that became too expensive earlier in the day. On the other hand, when a stock's price keeps running up on increasing volume during lunch, this indicates that it may be a real hottie with lots more moving to do—especially after 2:30 P.M. rolls around.

Price movements based on stock-specific developments

Two examples of stock-specific developments that trigger price movements are earnings announcements and stock splits. (See Chapter 6 for more on these and other recurring trends.)

Earnings announcements are the easier of the two to explain. When companies' quarterly earnings announcements are approaching and are expected to be favorable, their stock prices begin to climb up in anticipation of the good news. The price rise into earnings usually begins ten days to two weeks before the earnings announcement is scheduled to take place.

What's behind this trend? It's a case of traders following the classic rule "Buy the rumor, sell the news." This rule assumes that when the earnings news comes out, it already will have been factored into the price of the stock because, as long as there's no reason to expect bad news, traders *anticipate* good news and buy on the expectation that it will arrive (they buy the rumor). Whether or not good news ever arrives isn't important—the smart trader sells her position *before* the earnings announcement so that her profit won't be affected by the market's reaction, good or bad. Since many traders do this, the stock's price tends to drop toward the end of the last day of trading before the earnings announcement.

RULES OF THE GAME   Buy the rumor, sell the news.

Stock splits are a slightly weirder trend. When a company announces that a split will take place, the stock price tends to rise for a while. Since splits are usually announced one to three months in advance of the date the stock actually starts trading at the post-split price (the *ex-date*), this price movement tends to fizzle out after a few days, and the stock price returns to near its normal range. Then, one to two weeks before the split date, the price begins to rise again. In a bullish market, the price of the stock can rise significantly in the period before the split, and may continue to rise for a day or two afterward or may begin to drop on the day the stock begins to trade at the post-split price.

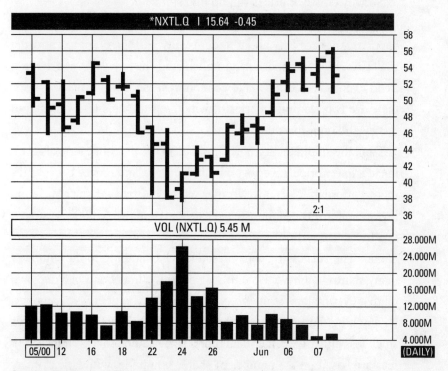

Stock split trend. NXTL's price rose over 35% in the two weeks preceding its two-for-one split (split ex-date of June 7 is indicated by the label "2:1").
Chart provided by TradePortal.com, Inc.

What's the explanation for this trend? In purely economic terms, it doesn't make any more sense than most professional stock analysts. *And you know how much they suck!* If you think about it for a couple of milliseconds, you'll realize that a stock split doesn't add any value whatsoever to the stock. Let's say Bland Corporation is going to split its stock two for one. If Bland is trading at $50 a share right before the split and then splits two for one, it will trade for $25 a share after the split but there will be twice as many Bland shares in the world. Someone who owns 100 shares of Bland at $50 before the split will own 200 shares at $25 afterward: twice the shares, each worth half as much. Since $100 \times \$50$ equals $200 \times \$25$, the value of the holding will not have changed by a cent. In fact, a split changes absolutely nothing about the value of the company.

So why do stock prices run up into splits?

As traders, we ultimately don't care what makes sense, only what happens. We care only about trader reality. Still, in order to know the trader reality, it's important to understand the *psychology* driving a trend even if it doesn't make economic sense. In the case of splits, there are two leading theories of why the price runs up—one stupid theory and one smart theory.

First, the stupid theory. The stupid theory is that if the stock is trading at a lower price, investors will find it more "attractive" because it's more "affordable." I have no idea what this means, since a $5000 investment in a two-dollar stock costs the same as a $5000 investment in a five-thousand-dollar stock—what matters is that you're investing $5000. The success of your investment has nothing to do with how many shares you have. It's either a good investment or a bad one, and all that ever matters is the *percentage return* you get on your money. (If anything, I'd think that having to buy more shares would make a stock less attractive rather than more, since some brokers' transaction fees are based on the number of shares you trade, with larger orders costing more—but *whatever*!) But maybe there are a lot of people out there in the investing public who find a cheaper stock more attractive and are more likely to buy it for that reason. Maybe the great interest in the stock created by its new cheapness will cause investors to pile in and drive the price up. Yeah, and maybe I'm a direct reincarnation of Queen Victoria. Who knows? Anything's possible!

On to the smarter theory. The smarter theory is a variation on "Buy the rumor, sell the news." According to the smarter theory, the fact that a company is splitting its stock is a good sign because it means the company thinks the stock price will keep going up. (By contrast, if you ever see a company doing a *reverse split*—making two shares into one at twice the price—stay away and don't even *think* about going there. The company is probably resorting to desperate measures to keep its stock price from dwindling into a submicroscopic state.) This would mean that the stock split announcement and the anticipation of the split is the rumor, and when the split finally happens it's the news—the news is that the split really happened and wasn't canceled. According to this theory, the price runs up not because of the split itself, but because of what the split means—that the company is optimistic about its stock's future prospects. In other words, the stock has *potential.* (Remember that word.)

I vote for the smarter theory.

Price runups in speculative stocks

Why was it that a stock like Amazon.com's just wouldn't stop gaining value in late 1998 and early 1999? Everyone seemed to agree that the stock price was irrational; the company was not earning money, and no one had any idea when it would. Yet it kept going up and up and up. Between January 1998 and March 1999, its price had increased by roughly fifteen times. Amazon was a tulip bulb, just like the tulip bulbs whose prices created the famous market bubble of eighteenth-century Holland. What is the market psychology that creates a tulip bulb phenomenon?

A few years ago I ran a successful sports memorabilia business, and I learned a lot about how perceptions in the market determine value. In my business, I sold baseball cards—especially cards in unopened wax packages. That's how I got the name "The Waxman," or Waxie. All this was at the height of the baseball-card market, when prices for desirable cards were going through the roof.

I learned that prices go up like rocket ships when people see huge *potential* but don't see any limit to it. What does that mean? Here's an example: Unopened wax packages of cards became very, very valuable. Why was that, when no one knew what was inside? The cards inside could end up to be really boring, common cards worth next to nothing. But what gets people going is the *possibility* that there's an incredibly valuable card inside. As long as people perceive *potential* in something and no one knows what it's really worth, it could be worth *infinity*—it *could*, it *could*, there's no denying that *it could*! A wax package *could* contain a one-of-a-kind flawed card that could be worth—well, for all anyone knows, infinity. Until someone opens the package, you just don't know!

I made a lot of money on those unknowns.

That's how it was with the original tulip bulbs, too. The reason they were so valuable was that in bulb form, no one could tell whether the flowers would be plain old boring tulips or unique variegated tulips of rare and irreproducible beauty. The *potential* for a bulb to produce a one-of-a-kind flower was enough to send its price into the stratosphere. Only when the plant actually bloomed would the true value of the bulb be known.

And that's how it was with Amazon. At the height of the Internet boom, everyone looked at Microsoft's and America Online's stock and saw how they had increased thousands of percent from their issue prices. If it could happen to those stocks, they figured, it could happen again—and everyone wanted to own the stock that would be *the next Microsoft*. Along came Amazon. Now, Amazon was a stock with *potential*, and no one knew what it was worth, since—because the company had no earnings yet—there was no objective data to base a valuation on. Here was a stock with potential, and as long as no one knew what it was worth, *it could be worth infinity*, just like Microsoft.

Once some objective information comes out that lets you calculate a valuation, though, it's all over—*poof!*—just like that. That's what finally stopped AOL's long price rise. When AOL announced earnings for the first time, its incredible run to infinity was over forever.

This is the kind of thinking that runs the market, and this is what you have to get in touch with if you want to understand and anticipate the market's moves.

Hot and cold sectors and sector rotation cycles

TRADER TALK   A *sector* is a subset of the market whose component companies are in the same general area of business.

As traders, we're not directly interested in how the NASDAQ and Dow are doing (though we are interested in how they can affect our trades). Instead, we're interested in the hot sector *du jour*. Even when the market as a whole isn't moving much, a discrete sector can be completely gonzo. When sectors really heat up, their cycles usually last for periods of one month to two years.

Hot sectors participate in marketwide rallies. Cold sectors don't. Even during major rallies, stocks in cold sectors trade in a range or even decline. That's why you need to keep track of sectors.

Even while a sector is in the hot phase of its cycle, it can cool off for brief periods during the run. For example, a sector can be on fire from November through March but within that period have occasional cold days or weeks while other sectors run or while it pulls back because traders are taking profits.

After a sector reaches its peak, its fall can occur much more quickly than its journey up. Sometimes the trip back down takes only half the amount of time the stock needed to go up, and sometimes even less than that. Whether you're an investor or a trader, you need to act fast when sector cycles end to avoid being crushed.

What makes a sector hot? During bull runs, it's the same thing that drives speculative stock—"tulips"—up and up. That thing is *potential*. Sectors that are perceived by the market to have *potential* can stay hot for as long as that sense of possibility remains untouched by some unfortunate reality or fact, such as hard evidence of a shrinking market for the companies' products.

During more bearish periods, sectors can remain in play if they are perceived to have something extra that gives them great value. For example, in such periods, semiconductor and fiber-optic stocks have done much better than e-tailers or online banks. This is because, while it is relatively easy for anyone—especially a traditional retailer or traditional bank—to set up an e-tailing business or online bank (and this ease has been those stocks' downfall), a semiconductor, Internet infrastructure, or fiber-optic company has unique proprietary technology. Others can't easily come in and start making the same or competitive products.

Objective common sense versus "trader reality"

It may be obvious to you that a stock or entire sector is overpriced and that irrational exuberance is at the wheel. This, however, should not have much effect on your trading decisions, because short-term trading has little to do with ultimate objective reality and everything to do with current—and transient—market perceptions.

For example, when you see that warm and fuzzy market darling FLUF's sales this year will be $400 *million* but the company has a market capitalization of over $70 *billion*, it's pretty obvious that a *lot* of good news—*far* into the future—has already been priced into the stock. Then you read an article concluding that the entire market for FLUF's product will be a mere $6.5 billion *three years from now*. Even if the company somehow managed to achieve a market share of

100 percent, the stock would still be selling at over ten times its total *sales*. Right now FLUF has roughly a 22 percent share of its market. It's unreasonable to expect that its market share will ever even get near 50 percent, but in any case, FLUF's valuation is beyond absurd.

In spite of that, just last week you saw an analyst recommend FLUF on CNBC because it's stealing business from its main competitor. It's obvious to you that even if FLUF stole *all* that competitor's business (which is next to impossible), its stock would *still* be trading at a ridiculous multiple. (Most companies are sold at five to seven times what their relative *earnings*—not *sales*—will be no more than five years into the future. A typical brick-and-mortar business will sell for no more than five to ten times *this year's* earnings.)

This FLUF recommendation is an egregious bit of nonsense. What you have to remember, though, is that trading is all about *perceptions*. That's why sensible valuations are *not* useful short-term trading tools. You can't just sell FLUF short and go away to Tahiti on vacation.

Ultimately, FLUF will reach its proper level, just as the e-tailers and online banks eventually did. Overvaluation may be the objective reality, and *eventually* common sense will win out and send overvalued shares lower. However, when the economy is booming, there will always be out-of-whack and inflated valuations because so much money is coming into the market.

The reason you can't simply sell FLUF short and head to Tahiti is that *trading reality is often different from objective reality and objective common sense.*

A stock could be trading at a ludicrous price by any standard; yet, as a trader, I might take this stock long for short periods and not think twice about it.

Why? It's because *the market is made up of traders*. Funds and institutions are all traders at heart. Today's overvalued stocks will eventually get to the few dollars a share they're really worth, but in the meantime, some weaselly analyst will give them upgrades based on the magic word that traders love to hear—*potential*. People are more afraid to miss rallies than they are to lose money when the market dies. As long as the *perception of potential* exists, the market can and will bounce and extend rallies for far longer than it should.

Reality dictates that a stock with a valuation of $9 billion on $450 million in sales plus slowing growth must at some point make its way down to what it's really worth. Trader reality, though, dictates that under the right circumstances it could go up by 100 percent before that happens. In a really nice rally, it could more than triple its current price. The trick for traders is not to worry much about the objective reality or what things *should* cost, but *only about trader reality*. That means you, as a trader, should look at the market in very small time frames and trade accordingly. You shouldn't worry about overvaluation *unless* the market's perception becomes the same as that overwhelming reality. And when it does, it's time for you to go short and ride overvalued stocks to their inevitable deaths.

A perception that the economy is getting better, that the bottom is near, and that things are turning around may make FLUF a great buy. A trader needs to be aware of the perception of the market and not worry much about valuations *until the market does*. Water seeks its own level, but at its own pace. Rather than becoming bears or bulls, traders should only be vigilant. Unless you are to become an investor (that most dreaded of fates), you must not get caught up in objective reality. And if you are an investor, you must know how to protect yourself by using put options or hedging.

Price movements based on technicals

Technical analysis of charts doesn't reveal anything fundamental about a company's value, its stock's real worth, or what ought to happen to the stock. It's merely a source of benchmarks that every competent trader is aware of. *That's why they work*: Everyone is looking at them, and everyone knows everyone else is looking at them, so they become important and everyone acts on them. That's why a moving stock will suddenly stop moving at 51, the price where it stopped before, even though in terms of fundamentals, 51 is a completely arbitrary number. That's also why the stock will not go below 38 unless things get really, really bad. The number 38 is nothing special; it's just that everyone knows the stock bounced upward at 38 before, so they'll look for it to do so again—because everyone else is.

Contrarian indicators

A contrarian indicator is an indicator that means the opposite of what it appears to mean. For traders, the best contrarian indicators are common and prevailing opinions that seem so solid that there's no way to argue people out of them. For example, when absolutely everyone starts to agree that the market will never stop going up, it's time for the good trader to start anticipating a market top. Likewise, when analysts try to call market bottoms in a correction, it's not yet time to start buying. It won't be time until analysts have *stopped* trying to call a bottom—when they've thrown up their hands and admitted that they don't know when the market will stop falling. This is like saying that the market could go down forever. And once everyone starts to think that the market will go down forever, it's time for the good trader to start to think about buying.

Why do contrarian indicators work? It's because, once *everyone* starts doing the same thing in the market in sync with the current trend, the trend can't survive. When the market is still anticipating a market top, there are still people who believe the market won't go up forever, and these people haven't bought into it yet. Once *everyone* becomes convinced the market will go on forever, though, everyone that's going to buy *will* buy, and after that happens, there will be no buyers left. *That's* when the market reaches its top. Likewise, in a correction, it's only when everyone starts to believe the market won't ever stop dropping—that belief being the contrarian indicator—that all the sellers will finally capitulate and sell, and this capitulation is the only thing that will exorcise the selling demon from the market.

Chapter 5

The Seven Deadly Sins, Plus Fear

Knowing Your Psychological Achilles' Heel

....
This chapter covers:

- Why traders are their own worst enemies
- Eight psychological pitfalls that cause traders to fail consistently
- How to identify the pitfalls that are hindering your success
- Why your goal should be not perfection but control of emotional barriers to success
- How long-term trading success is achieved through consistency
- How to approach each new trade with a positive attitude

You Are Your Own Worst Enemy

History repeats itself. This is nowhere more true than in the market.

As we said in the last chapter, the market is not so much full of mysterious surprises as it is full of predictable trends and repeated patterns. And the reason it's predictable is that everything that happens is a result of the motivations of the people in the market. It's all based on the principles of human nature you learned in grade school.

The market is not the only thing that's predictable or the only thing that functions according to the principles of human nature. There's another factor in your trading that acts according to these principles. That factor is *you*.

You, as a trader, are your own worst enemy. That's because you—like every trader—have psychological and emotional soft spots, Achilles' heels, that can cause you to make the same mistakes again and again without ever realizing it. The difference between a successful trader and a failing trader is that the successful trader has recognized his or her psychological Achilles' heels and has learned to control them so they don't undermine trading and sabotage success.

Lots of people say that the two things that drive the market are greed and fear. On the simplest level, this is true. Greed is what makes people buy, and fear is what makes people sell. And greed and fear are two things that can actually benefit a trader. Greed in reasonable doses, or at least the desire to earn money, is what motivates us to get involved in the market in the first place and make successes of ourselves. Fear can be a healthy response when we sense danger or disaster closing in. It motivates us to get out of a situation that could ruin us.

But when they get out of control, greed and fear are two of the psychological pitfalls that make traders fail. There are six others. I call the whole list "the seven deadly sins, plus fear." Many traders can identify several of these psychological and emotional weak spots by studying trading mistakes that they've made. All of them can ruin you. For example, pride is an especially deadly sin that prevents you from feeling a healthy fear and getting out of a position that will sink you. Wrath and other emotional stresses from your personal life can take away the healthy desire to succeed in the market. Lust, gluttony, and envy are specific forms of greed. And sloth just makes you a lazy, sloppy trader who can't win.

Traders who consistently fail make mistakes that fall into one or more of these eight categories. Look over the list and see how many you can identify as causes for trades that have taken you to Disasterville.

The Seven Deadly Sins of Trading, Plus Fear

1. Greed. As I discuss below, the desire to make money is what motivates us to become successful traders in the first place, and this is a good thing. But the desire to succeed is different from the deadly sin of greed, which is the sin of trying to get every last cent out of a trade. This kind of reckless greed makes traders hold on to their positions long after the downside has started to outweigh the upside and risk outweighs potential reward.

Here's an example. The greedy trader sees that BUXX is starting on a run; it's reported good news and is already up 20 percent for the day, but the volume is still building, it's stable at the current price, the market is rallying strongly, and it looks like BUXX will go higher. Greedster buys 1000 shares of BUXX at $6 a share. By 12:15 P.M., the stock has raced up to $10—a gain of over 66 percent for the day, and a profit of $4000 on 1000 shares.

Greedster knows perfectly well that round numbers like 10 are psychological barriers for traders, and that if a stock is going to put on the brakes, it will probably be near a point like this. Sure enough, after momentarily shooting to $10.03, the price stops rising and starts to go down. Greedster knows that he should get out now and rebuy later, but he keeps thinking, What if it goes to 12 before it stops? What if it makes a 100 percent gain? How will I ever forgive myself for missing out on another $2000 profit because I got out too soon?

So, of course what ends up happening is that BUXX drops down to $9.50 and then $8.75, ending the day at $8.90. The next day the market opens on a sour note and Greedster is lucky to get out at $8.70, down $1300 from the profit he could have had.

The way to get around the lure of greed is to take profits religiously. *Just take them!* It doesn't matter if the stock goes up another dollar or two after you're out of the position. The important thing is that you've made a clean profit and are ready to go on to the next trade with even more capital than you had before. And going on to the next trade is better than staying in the old one once it's gotten too risky, because the next trade will have an upside that outweighs the downside (if it didn't, you wouldn't have any reason to get into the position at all, no?), while the old trade's downside has begun to outweigh any further gains you're likely to make.

RULES OF THE GAME   Lock in profits religiously. *No one ever went broke taking profits!*

RULES OF THE GAME   Greed = Death. *Pigs get slaughtered!*

RULES OF THE GAME   Swing for singles, not the fences—and often you'll hit home runs anyway.

   2. *Pride.* The weakness of pride must have cost thousands of people millions of dollars in the year 2000 alone. This trading sin is all about the refusal to take small losses on a bad trade and *get out*. Another word for it is plain old stubbornness. Why do people resist taking small losses and moving on to better trades? It's because they don't want to admit that their decision to get into a position was anything less than brilliant. They don't want to admit that they were wrong about the stock. ·

   I don't know about you, but I think it's ridiculous and completely counterproductive to expect yourself to be right about everything you do. *Hello! Reality check!* How can any mature person pretend to be right all the time? To me, this is childish and really, really silly. The mature person realizes that she's going to be right some of the time and wrong some of the time. She tries to be right as much as possible, but when she's wrong she admits it right away, to herself and anyone else concerned, gets over it, and moves on in the right direction. It's much easier to move past your mistakes and learn from them if you don't keep living them for extra days, weeks, or months!

Example: The prideful trader plops down $10,000 for 500 shares of Ambiguity Incorporated at $20 a share. He believes that the concept behind Ambiguity's innovative new software is going to be the Next Big Thing, and he's seen a lot of reliable information that backs up this idea. The price has recently moved up steadily, from 16 to 20. And it's true that buying AMBI is not all an unreasonable trade.

For some reason, though, the new concept is slow to catch on. Prideful holds AMBI for three weeks and sees its share price remain essentially the same as where he bought it. It goes up a dollar, down a dollar, and so on—it's trading in a range and doesn't show any signs of movement. Then the market turns ugly and all the tech stocks go down. AMBI doesn't tank quickly, but over the next couple of weeks it gradually sinks back to $16 a share. There's no volume, and it seems that no one is interested in the stock.

Prideful insists that if he just keeps holding AMBI, it will not only recover but bring him a large profit once the market catches on to its value. He holds the stock for the next five months, watching it move up and down between 15 and 16. Finally, after more than six months, the stock goes on a run—up to 22. Prideful does the right thing and takes profits at this level. Now he can have the last word with all his friends, who were sure he would never make a cent on the stock. He gets to say to everyone, "I told you this thing would be hot eventually!"

But who cares? The reality is that Prideful has tied up $10,000 for six months for a 10 percent profit when he could have made at least that much every week or so by moving on to better trades. There was no compelling reason to think AMBI would go up soon, and Prideful had no exit plan.

And the really scary thing is that AMBI could just as easily have gone to 6!

RULES OF THE GAME   Take small losses.

RULES OF THE GAME   You don't need to win on every trade.

RULES OF THE GAME   Don't marry stocks.

3. Lust. The problem here is sexy stocks. You know what I mean: the sector *du jour*, the hot stock everybody's talking about, the one that makes you feel like a winner if you own it and like a loser if you don't—whether the trade makes sense or not.

People chase these hotties because they feel they just have to have them. And a similar thing happens when any stock suddenly goes on a run: People see that it's popular, want to be part of the action (whatever that means), and end up chasing the stock as its price runs up and paying so much for it that the trade can't possibly work out.

This behavior is pure emotion, not thought. This is your inner knucklehead at work.

RULES OF THE GAME   Don't chase a stock; wait for it to come to you. *Last one in the pool swims with the turd!*

RULES OF THE GAME   Control your inner knucklehead.

Here's an example of what not to do. Let's say you've been following Slam Executables, Inc. (SEXY), which is in a hot sector and just announced a stock split. SEXY is now at 18, and you figure it could get to 25 or more by the time of the split. The market is bullish, and it looks like a great trade.

The problem is that SEXY has been going up for the past four days. It started at 12, but you didn't notice it until it hit 18—a 50 percent increase—and it's still rising. The stock split is a month away, and you know it's pretty likely to cool off for a while between now and the split. Still, everyone is talking about SEXY and the executables sector, and what if it just goes on a tear and becomes the next blockbuster stock? You'd just die if you missed the boat like that. And besides, you want to be able to tell people that you hold a position in SEXY.

So you load up on SEXY at $18.50 and settle down to wait with 1000 shares.

During the next two weeks, SEXY goes to 19 and change, then levels off, loses steam, and drifts down to 17. Then a couple of leading NASDAQ companies give earnings warnings, the market tanks, and SEXY slides to 15, triggering the stop you'd set at 16 on half your holdings. The stock trades in a range for a week, then begins to rise into the split. Your plan is to sell a day or two after the split. SEXY rises a little beyond $20.50 by the second day after the split, and then the volume dries up and you sell it for a $2 profit. But since you stopped out of half your shares at 16, you lost $2.50 per share on that half, with a net loss of .50 on 500 shares.

What went wrong?

What went wrong was that *you didn't let the stock come to you*. Instead, you chased it as its price rose, knowing perfectly well that—following the stock split trend—it would probably pull back before running up again.

You knew that it was more likely to pull back than it was to continue on an uninterrupted run to 25, and you knew that if you bought at 18 or higher you were probably paying too much. You disregarded what you knew was more probable in favor of what *might* happen—even if there was only a very small chance of that unlikely thing happening. You should have given the stock a chance to *come to you*, at a price you felt was reasonable. If the stock had pulled a surprise and never gotten down to where you thought it would, that would be okay—there were many other stocks to trade, and some of them would have come down to your price. You didn't *have* to own SEXY. In two months, no one but you would have cared (even now, no one but you really cares), and you don't want the reason you care to be because a stock has lost you a bagful of money.

What was the right way to play SEXY?

When the market is bullish, it's very likely for a stock to rise when a split is announced, drift down after a few days' rally, and then begin to rise again a week or so before the split. If that's the trend and there's no solid reason to think the stock will shoot to the moon immediately, you should wait a few days for the stock to drift down and stabilize before buying it. If you had done this with SEXY, you could have bought it at $16.50 and then sold it for $20.50, for a $4.00 profit on the entire 1000 shares. If you had a solid reason to think the stock might continue to rally, you could have bought half the total number of shares you wanted at a price that might have turned out to be too high, and waited for a lower price to buy the other half. If it had turned out to be too high, it would only have reduced your profit.

WAXIE'S STREET SMARTS

No stock goes up or down in a straight line. Wait for a pullback before buying.

You must use the same strategy during an intraday rally. Since rallying stocks often pull back during the lunch hour (1:00 to 2:30 P.M. Eastern time), that's often a good time to enter the trade. It's really frustrating to buy a stock too high, only to watch it dip and then have to make its way back up to where you bought it so that you can finally begin to think about maybe making some money on it.

And the same thing goes for selling short, except in reverse. Don't chase the stock down to short it. Instead, wait for it to bounce up a bit before you enter the position.

4. *Envy.* Envyman spends a lot of energy focusing on what other traders do (or *say* they do). He then gets himself all tied up knots worrying that everybody else is making 30 percent a week on

their portfolio, that everybody else finds great stocks that he misses, and that everybody else knows what they're doing while he doesn't. This leads him to try to copy what he thinks others are doing, doing it too late, and doing things that aren't good ideas in the first place. He gets so confused trying to keep track of so many stocks that he doesn't understand what's going on with any of them. *If you chase too many rabbits, they'll all get away!* It also leads him to—yes—commit the sin of Lust and chase stocks as their price runs up instead of letting the stocks come to him.

NEWBIE TRAP   If you chase too many rabbits, they'll all get away.

Envyman doesn't realize that a lot of what people say is either a big exaggeration or complete bulldinky. He doesn't understand that whatever it is, his job is to treat it as though it's complete bulldinky. He doesn't realize that for every smart trader there are hundreds of wanna-bes, incompetents, and simpletons.

A close cousin to envy is competitiveness. Some traders want to show everyone that they're the best, the smartest, the baddest. They need to ask themselves: What is the point of this exercise— to play a competitive game or to make money? Your focus should be on making money. If you're in it for the competition, you should play some other game. The only reason to trade is to make money, and if your mind is on some imaginary competition that only you care about, you'll never make money.

The smart trader ignores idle hype, rumors, and boasting, and uses his or her own knowledge and judgment to find trades that make sense and that he has confidence in. This doesn't mean he ignores the current buzz—because that market noise sometimes leads to good trading opportunities. But he knows what it's reasonable to expect from his trading and how to achieve it without worrying about what everyone else is doing.

5. ***Gluttony.*** The Gluttoness is a victim of her own success. She's had such good luck with a certain type of stock that she just can't

get enough of it, and she ends up overexposing her portfolio to one stock or sector.

Sectors tend to move together, and often one sector will move down as another one moves up. Sectors are cyclical, which means that they go through hot and cold phases. No one stock or type of stock is hot all the time, and when a leading stock in a sector gets into trouble, it tends to bring all the rest down with it.

The Gluttoness bought some biotech stocks just as a huge sector run was beginning. She bought BioGem Therapeutics and Radgene, Inc., saw what powerhouses they were as they climbed 40 percent apiece, and loaded up on BioMiracle, BioSalvation, and Hallelujah Genetics. To do this, she closed out all her other positions, which had been in technology companies and a few traditional blue chip stocks.

The trouble was that, two days later, the leading U.S. biotech company announced that it didn't believe it could become profitable for another ten years. The whole biotech sector tanked bigtime in premarket trading, leaving the Gluttoness with worse than an empty plate when she was forced to sell all her biotech stocks at large losses.

Diversification is important even for short-term traders. Some market moves can't be protected against, and if all your holdings are in one or a few sectors, you are vulnerable and just begging for a ticket to Disasterville.

WAXIE'S STREET SMARTS

Don't concentrate your holdings in one or only a few sectors. Spread them around so they aren't all vulnerable to the same market events.

6. *Sloth.* Traders don't do any work, right? They just log on and start making money by watching the prices go up and down, right?

Wrong, wrong, wrong! That's only true if you're talking about *losing* traders. Slothful, lazy traders are certain to become losing traders, even if they luck out for a little while. Lazy traders neglect to research and monitor stocks, so they haven't a clue what's going on with their stocks or why. Slothful traders haven't done enough thinking to have a plan, and trading without a plan is one of the surest ways to lose in the market.

The lazy trader might buy a stock, MOJO, because he sees that it's been going up steadily for a week and a half. He doesn't know why, but he does know MOJO is a "strong" stock and figures you can't argue with success, or some such nonsense. He buys it in the morning, it goes up a few percentage points, and he figures he's one smart dude.

To his surprise, MOJO does a complete one-eighty in the afternoon and starts going down as steadily as it went up in the morning. The lazy trader can't figure out what's wrong. Why did MOJO lose its mojo? If he'd just bothered to check the earnings calendar, he'd have seen that the company was scheduled to report earnings that day after the market closed. The steady runup was in anticipation of the earnings announcement, and now traders were taking profits and getting out of the stock in case of a negative reaction to the earnings results.

What's the lesson here? It's that you must:

- know why a stock is moving

- know why you're buying a stock

- check basic information on the stock

- once you're in the position, watch the market, check for news on the stock and its sector, and monitor the stock's behavior throughout the day

- know what events are coming up for the company so you can anticipate changes in the stock's direction

If you blow off these tasks, you'll be unpleasantly surprised, and quite frankly, you'll deserve it. Think about your dreams and what you're trying to accomplish by trading. Is it important to you? If it is, put in the work to make it happen and make your dreams come true.

7. ***Wrath.*** This is the most purely emotional sin for a trader. I use wrath to represent any emotional stress that is making you have a bad day.

Here, the rule is simple: If you're sick, if your dog died or your wife left you, or even if you just got up on the wrong side of the bed, *don't trade*. Just do something else that day or for as many days as it takes to calm down. Take a break. Take a walk. Enjoy the sunshine if the weather's nice, or curl up with a good book or video if it's not.

The reason? If you trade when you're not feeling well, physically or emotionally, you won't trade well. You'll just lose money. You may even become self-destructive, do things that don't make sense, and find yourself losing almost intentionally. At the very least, you'll be too distracted to trade successfully.

RULES OF THE GAME   On a bad day, take a walk.

Knowing when not to trade is an important form of discipline you *must* learn. This discipline is also necessary on days when the market is so directionless and choppy that no trade is going to go anywhere and you'll only churn your account if you try to trade. But the main point here is to be in good enough touch with your inner state that you can recognize when your mood is a danger to your account's well-being. In any case, it's healthy to get away from the market for a day or two, or even a few weeks, from time to time. The time away will help you regain perspective about what things in life really matter. And if you *need* to trade every day, it may be a sign of an unhealthy addiction.

RULES OF THE GAME   You don't have to trade every day.

8. Fear. Fear is one of the classic motivators of the market, and it has a valuable purpose: to prevent you from doing something incredibly dangerous and self-destructive. But too much fear is not healthy, and paradoxically, it will cause you to do things that are dangerous and self-destructive: specifically, panic buying and panic selling.

Panic buying and panic selling were the sins I kept committing when I was Mr. Loser. I'd buy stocks, see them go down, panic-sell them at a loss, watch them turn around and go back up, panic-buy them once they'd gone too high, watch them turn around and fall, panic-sell at a loss, and on and on until I had lost most of my money. Instead of buying low and selling high, I was doing just the opposite—buying high and selling low. This is a sure ticket to Disasterville.

The two cures for this problem are, first, to have a plan and stick to it and, second, to control the fear that drives your inner knucklehead to self-defeating actions.

RULES OF THE GAME   Plan the trade and trade the plan.

The very worst way to trade is emotionally, outside your plan. Instead of giving in to emotion, know what you're going to do, have good reasons for it, and stick to your plan. A good plan will include alternatives so you'll know what to do in several different foreseeable situations. Stick to your plan unless there's a damn solid reason not to—not because you're panicking.

Which Pitfalls Are Hindering Your Success?

If you want to improve as a trader, you must identify the mistakes you make consistently so that you can recognize your own psychological Achilles' heels. To do this, look back at ten losing trades you've made in the last few weeks. Can you find similarities? Look closely and be brutally honest with yourself. Part of being a good trader is being able to look at things with a clear eye and seeing what's really there, not what you *wish* was there.

Now here's the tough part: Look back at your recent *successful* trades and find the ones that succeeded only by luck. How would they have turned out if you hadn't been lucky? What were your mistakes with these trades?

Identify the two most common mistakes you make. Identify your most disastrous trades and identify the mistakes you made with them.

From now on, you must keep your psychological and emotional soft spots in mind at all times while you're trading. It may sound silly, but I often put little Post-its with phrases like "Greed = Death" on my computer—so I can constantly remind myself.

Your Goal Is Not Perfection but Self-Control

Your goal as a trader should not be to trade perfectly all the time, to win on every trade, or to be perfect in any other way. Putting too much pressure on yourself to be perfect is one of the best ways to make lots of mistakes. Besides the fact that no one can be perfect, there's also the fact that *you don't need to be perfect.* Why bother with all that stress? You can make amazing amounts of money in the market by being a good, consistent trader.

Think about a baseball team. Not every player can set records, be Most Valuable Player, or have the highest salary in the league. In fact, even the best hitters in baseball get hits only a third of the time. I'd be happy if I could just play major league baseball and do my job consistently and well. That would be reward enough. As a trader, you'll be richly rewarded if you do your job consistently and well. You'll be doing far better than 99 percent of the other people trading stocks in the market, not to mention money managers, analysts, and other Wall Street charlatans.

Instead of perfection, your goal should be to control the emotional barriers to your success. That and learning to follow all the Rules of the Game are the two most important things you can do to improve yourself as a trader.

Long-term trading success is achieved through consistency: consistently taking small losses and larger profits, consistently rejecting trades that are too risky or that aren't based on good reasoning, and consistently doing what you know is right instead of acting against your better judgment. Consistency is a discipline, and it will serve you well in life as well as in trading.

Play to Win!

The purpose of identifying your psychological soft spots is not to make you feel like you're a bad trader. All traders, even the best, have Achilles' heels—they just recognize and control them. Instead, the purpose of getting to know your soft spots is to develop a realistic sense of your strengths and weaknesses so that you can recognize mistakes before they happen. Being realistic and clear-eyed—about yourself, and about the market and the trades you make—is the way to succeed as a trader.

If you make a mistake, or if your emotions get the better of you on a trade—if, as they say in the recovery movement, you have a "slip"—don't beat yourself up over it. What's the point? That just makes the mistake last longer. Don't think about "making up" for the bad trade. It's old history, and it's dead and gone. Besides, putting pressure on yourself to "make up" for a mistake will probably lead you to force trades when you shouldn't. Instead, learn from the experience and move on to the next trade with a fresh and positive attitude. *Always play to win!*

RULES OF THE GAME   Play to win!

Part III

Playing
to Win

Chapter 6

Making Friends with the Trends

The Right Way to Pick Stocks

This chapter covers:

- Why the best short-term trading strategy is to identify market trends
- Two things you must know about any trade before making it
- Five strong market trends:
    - Earnings
    - Stock splits
    - News
    - Short-selling weak stocks that have risen on news
    - Hot sectors/sympathy plays
- Additional tradable trends
- How to trade IPOs

TRADER TALK A *trend* is a pattern that is repeated by different stocks and can be relied on to reasonably predict the price movements of similar stocks.

The Trend Is Your Best Friend

Trend trading is the best way I've found to pick stocks and make money in the market—any market. The market contains hundreds of trends—recurring price-movement patterns—and all you have to do is look for them. As you read in the last chapter, as long as *people* are in charge of trading decisions, trends will arise because people are creatures of habit who tend to repeat patterns. Think about the person who's in charge of trading in and out of equity positions for a big mutual fund. Let's say it's a guy named Eric who lives on the Upper West Side of Manhattan and works in the Times Square area. Every morning Eric, a disgustingly energetic guy, gets up at 6 A.M. and goes to the gym, where he does half an hour on the treadmill followed by a circuit of weight machines. On his way home he stops at the corner deli to pick up a bagel and a cup of coffee. He goes back to his apartment, showers, shaves, and dresses, and walks down Broadway to the subway and takes the number 9 train to work. The people at the gym, the deli, and the subway station could practically set a clock by Eric, and anyone interested in breaking into his apartment could watch him for a few days and see the best times to do it. Of course, there are days when Eric is on vacation or sick or was out too late the night before and doesn't get up at 6. But he follows the same routine over 90 percent of the time.

Because they're acted on by humans, stocks and the market as a whole develop habits, too. These patterns of behavior are trends, and just as a burglar would do well to watch Eric's patterns for a break-in opportunity, we can watch stocks for trends that will give us good trading opportunities.

Trends are the bread and butter of my trading. There are so many of them that there will always be some operating, whether the market is in a bull or bear phase. Trends are also important because when I see one operating, I know I can't trade against it. That's like trying to swim against a strong current—it's foolish, and it just won't work.

WAXIE'S STREET SMARTS

Don't try to buck the trend.

Trends are your friends. Like your friends, they'll lend you a helping hand most of the time—but there will also be times when they'll let you down. We understand that our friends aren't perfect and we forgive them, and it should be the same with trends. In fact, it's good for a trend *not* to work all the time—because if anything worked 100 percent of the time, it would become obvious to everyone, and people would start to change their behavior to try to increase their advantage. And once their behavior changed, the trend wouldn't be able to work anymore.

In fact, that's exactly what happens to trends that become well recognized. In general, *once a trend is known by too many people, it no longer works.*

Before we look at how to use trends to pick stocks to trade, you must know what two things you have to figure out about any trade before making it.

Two Things You Must Know about a Trade

No matter what your reason is for picking a stock—because of a trend, based on technical analysis of charts, or because you're an investor who bases decisions on company fundamentals—there are two things you have to think about. These two things must be part of your decision-making process on every trade you ever make. If you discipline yourself to always ask these two questions and avoid the trade if you get a wrong answer, you're well on your way to becoming a successful trader.

The two things you must ask yourself about every trade are *whether you have a compelling reason to believe the trade will work* and *what is the trade's risk-to-reward ratio.*

Is there a compelling reason to believe the trade will work?

Before buying any stock, you must be able to articulate a solid reason to believe its value will rise in the immediate future. If you're shorting, you must have a good reason to believe its value will drop.

Some traders get into positions for reasons that would make me laugh if I were a meaner person. I've actually heard people say they bought stocks because they "wanted to see what the stock would do," they "like" the company, they think the stock is "due for a breakout," or they think—*get this!*—that it would be "a fun stock to own."

A fun stock to own? Yo, homie, you need to get out more! If you want to own something fun, do what I do and go buy yourself some interesting toys. I know what's fun and what's not, and losing money on a stock is not fun. Besides, stocks are for making money, not for owning. *Use 'em and abuse 'em!*

As for the other non-reasons, well, let's see. "Wanting to see what a stock will do" sounds to me like gambling—throw some money at it and see if you win or lose. A gambling mentality has no place in trading—it's as sure a way to lose as eating two-week-old sushi is a sure way to get sick. As for "liking" a company, that's just naive. The company doesn't like you, its management and board of directors don't like you, and emotions like that have no place in trading. You should like your friends and maybe your neighbors or coworkers, but it makes no sense to "like" a company that's basically in the business of making money off you. Instead, you should treat it as the money-making creature that it is and try to make some money back from it. *Use it and abuse it!* The company and its management want your money. You should want whatever money it will give you. If you like its product, then by all means buy it and enjoy it—*knock yourself out!*—but don't get confused and think that means you should also buy the stock.

Finally, some traders buy beaten-down stocks that they think are "due for a breakout." This isn't quite as wacked a reason as some of the others people give. But it's still not a good one.

Think about it this way: if you were managing a baseball team and had to choose a pinch hitter, would you rather use a consistently good hitter with a .370 batting average or a weak hitter with a .100 average who *might* be "due for a hit"? Which obviously makes more sense? Go with the strategy that has the best chance of success. Don't play maybes!

RULES OF THE GAME Don't play maybes. *When in doubt, stay out!*

If you always use sound reasoning to pick stocks and always have a good reason for a trade, there are other benefits as well. For instance, you'll be much less inclined to purchase a stock impulsively or to get into a play on the basis of a "hot tip."

I never make a trade unless I absolutely believe it will be a winner. I know that some trades are stronger than others, and I put more money into the strong ones and less into the weaker ones, but *I never go into a trade not knowing whether it will work.* Why would I make a trade I don't think will work? Of course, I'm not always right—no one is—but I'm right a lot more than I'm wrong because I make only the trades I have good, solid reasons to believe in. And, because I know some trades won't work out but don't know which ones because I only make trades I believe in, I set stops on *all* my trades to keep from losing much on the ones that don't work out.

So, the first thing you must always ask yourself before making a trade is whether you have a sound reason for thinking it will work.

RULES OF THE GAME Always have a good reason. *No reason, no play!*

What is the trade's risk-to-reward ratio?

The second thing you must always ask yourself about before you make a trade is this: What is its risk-to-reward ratio? In other words, what's the likely return on the trade if it goes according to plan, and how much are you likely to lose if it doesn't?

For a trade to make sense, its potential reward must outweigh its potential loss, and by as much as possible. Obviously, if a trade is more likely to fail than succeed, *don't go there*. If the trade is equally likely to succeed or fail, it's no better than a coin flip. Don't make that trade, either.

If success is only slightly more likely than failure, you're at least on the right side of the risk-to-reward ratio, but is it really worth it? If there's no good trading opportunity in sight, just wait.

How do you figure out the potential reward and potential risk? This is something you always need to do, since you shouldn't be getting into a trade unless you have a plan, and your plan will be based on what you think will happen. You'll anticipate reward based on the strength of the stock, the outcome of similar trades made on other stocks for the same reason (the trend), market conditions, and technical and psychological resistance levels you see for the stock. If you want to trade Bull Run, Inc. (TORO) based on a trend you've observed in four other stocks (so you have a good, compelling reason for the play), you'll judge TORO's strength (it's a leader in its sector that always has good earnings and tends to run up strongly during market rallies), look up the range of percentage returns those other stocks gave (between 8 percent and 22 percent), market conditions (becoming more bullish), and resistance levels for TORO (right now it's trading at 18; it's got technical resistance at around 23, and although a little psychological resistance may appear at 20, it'll be more of an issue at 25 and certainly at 30).

A 10 percent rise in TORO's price would bring it to a little under 20. Since the stock and the market are strong and four other stocks have given good returns on this play, and since the stock has been as high as 23 before, it's reasonable to anticipate that, unless the market turns sour, the stock could see 23 if it goes on a strong run. That would be a return of over 25 percent. It looks like the potential return on this play is somewhere between 10 percent and 25 percent, with a decent likelihood that the return will be at the higher end.

And what's the potential loss? That depends on where you set your stops, which depends on all the things discussed in Chapter 9. Let's say you don't think TORO is likely to go down past 17, since the chart shows strong support there. If you set your stop just below 17 and it ends up being triggered, your loss will be about 6 percent. That's kind of high, but since it looks very unlikely that the stock will head down that far, the risk of loss is actually not large.

So TORO gives you a probable upside of at least 10 percent and as much as 25 percent with a relatively unlikely downside of 6 percent. This is a good risk-to-reward ratio.

If you have a good reason for every trade you make, and make only trades with risk-to-reward ratios that are solidly favorable, you're playing to win and you will win.

RULES OF THE GAME   Play to win!

Five Strong Market Trends

There are countless large and small trends in the market, but some are stronger and more stable than others. The following five trends are stable in the appropriate market environment and give a good overview of the sorts of patterns that exist in the market.

Earnings

The earnings trend is one of the strongest trends there is. When a company is expected to have good earnings (to see analysts' true expectations of a company's earnings, find out the earnings "whisper number"), its stock usually begins to rise in price, starting about two weeks before the earnings announcement is scheduled to take place. A stock's price can go up as much as 50 percent to 100 percent or more in anticipation of a good earnings report.

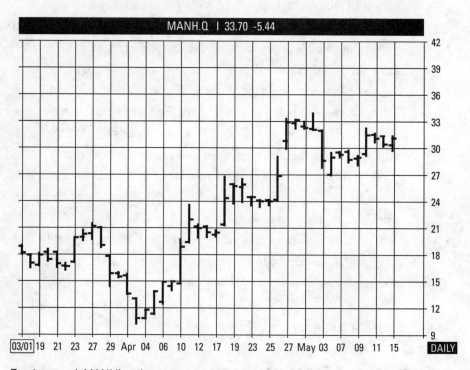

Earning trend. MANH's price rose over 160 percent in the three weeks preceding its earnings announcement on April 26.
Chart provided by TradePortal.com, Inc.

Of course, if a company gives an earnings warning, its stock may not be as good a candidate for the earnings-run play. In the right market environment, though, the earnings trend may work in spite of everything.

For me, the *only* way to trade an earnings run is to *always, always, always sell the stock before the earnings announcement*. Percentagewise, *holding a stock through its earnings announcement is a losing play.* Stocks often drop like stones right after earnings are announced, even if the report is good, because the good news was fully priced into the stock before the announcement. *Remember, buy the rumor, sell the news!* Stocks *occasionally* continue to climb after earnings, but if you were to consistently hold over earnings, you'd lose money *many* more times than not, and that's a loser's game. And your losses would be large, because most companies announce earnings either after the market closes or before the market opens, so prices can plummet in premarket trading and you'll have no way to escape the devastation. In fact, I usually sell early because stocks sometimes start to sell off toward the end of the last day before the earnings announcement.

Always remember that your goal is to take control of your money. *Never leave it in a situation over which you have no control.* Since you have absolutely no control over the earnings report a company will give, you should never, *never* hold over earnings.

WAXIE'S STREET SMARTS

Always sell a stock before it announces earnings.

RULES OF THE GAME   Buy the rumor, sell the news.

Stock splits

Another strong and lasting trend is for the stock of a company that's announced a stock split to run up into the split's ex-date. Though the inherent value of a company is not literally enhanced by a stock split, as discussed in Chapter 4, stocks that are about to split will typically outperform the market. Although this pattern usually begins ten days to two weeks before the stock's ex-date, it's a good idea to wait for the stock to start to ramp up before entering a position. The runup will generally continue into the ex-date and sometimes for a day or two beyond it. Key indicators of how to play the split can usually be found by checking out how other stocks that have recently split trended into their splits. As always, use protective and trailing stops. That way, if the market turns against you or the stock isn't ready to run, you can always jump out with a small loss and then jump back later in if the situation warrants.

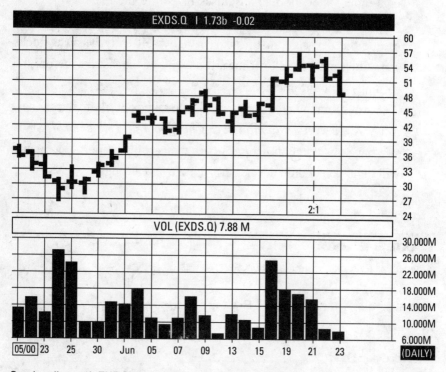

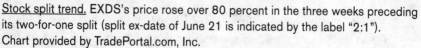

Stock split trend. EXDS's price rose over 80 percent in the three weeks preceding its two-for-one split (split ex-date of June 21 is indicated by the label "2:1"). Chart provided by TradePortal.com, Inc.

You can find information on upcoming and past splits on the splits calendars at Web sites like TrendFund.com or Yahoo! Finance (http://biz.yahoo.com/c/s.html). Bear in mind that Yahoo!'s accuracy varies. Although *splits calendars* give a number of dates, the ex-date is the only important one. Some calendars include a "record date," which is as irrelevant as a freezer at the South Pole.

When choosing stocks to play for splits, make sure the split ratio is at least two shares for one. Generally, a larger ratio (such as three for one or even four for one) indicates a stronger split runup. Splits in ratios such as three for two don't have large price movements into their splits. And *never, ever* touch a stock that's doing a reverse split (such as one for four). Reverse splits are usually desperate attempts by failing companies to bolster their dwindling stock prices. Avoid them like a disease.

TRADER TALK   The *ex-date* is the day a stock's share price changes to reflect a stock split and revised numbers of shares are credited to shareholders' accounts.

News

Beautiful mad runs in stock prices are often triggered by good news, either about the company itself or about another company in its sector if the sector is a hot one. The key to participating in price runs started by news is to get in early, before everyone else has. If you're the last one in, you'll buy at the highest price and then watch the stock price go down. Is *that* any way to trade?

Likewise, bad news can send a stock's price plummeting into hell-fire. And, like everything else in the market, what actually matters is not whether the news is really and truly good or bad, but *whatever the market perceives it to be.* You might not think the market's reaction to a piece of news makes any sense, but what *you* think is irrelevant to your trading. *Always go with the market.*

Why is it sometimes possible to make money trading when news comes out, even though the Rules of the Game say to buy the rumor and sell the news? It's possible because, in these cases, there was no rumor. Since the news that came out wasn't expected, there was no period leading up to the news in which its value was priced into the stock. And the news gives the stock that magic glow of *potential*.

The primary trend concerning news is that *news trumps other trends*. What does this mean?

Let's say you're holding Da Bomb Co. into its upcoming split. BOMB really is the bomb—a winning company in a hot sector, going into a rare four-for-one split. *You go, Co.!* The play is going really nicely, and the ex-date is three days away.

The next morning, you see unexpected news that business in BOMB's sector has dropped off sharply in the last quarter and that this slowdown is projected to continue for at least the next six months. What's going to happen to the split run? *News trumps other trends.* Unless the market decides it doesn't care about this news (which is *not* likely), Da Bomb's run is over. You have to get out of the stock, because if you don't, *this baby gonna explode in yo face.* When important news comes out, abandon other trends. Unexpected news is one of the main reasons why you must set stops on every trade.

In the same way, if you've sold short to ride a trend in which stocks usually go down, significant good news about the stock should send it buzzing back up.

Keep in mind that, unless the market is completely bonkers, only real, substantial news will have much effect on the stock or the trend. Trivial news or ho-hum news releases put out by the company usually won't. *Your job is to judge how the market is going to judge the news.*

Next let's look at an example of a shortable trend.

Short-Selling Weak Stocks That Have Risen on News

In both bull and bear markets, stocks can become targets for shorting (see Chapter 10) as a result of trends. Shorting is always a stronger strategy during a bearish phase, but many short plays work extremely well in bull markets—in fact, some shorting opportunities don't even arise in bear markets because many shortable trends are the after-effects of buyable trends.

An example is the extremely reliable trend of weak stocks falling like overripe fruit after they have run up on so-so news. Let's say the biotech sector has been red-hot during the last couple of weeks. Every tiny, one-trick company that puts out news about an FDA Phase I trial (the most preliminary stage of testing) has been running up 40 percent to 200 percent.

Now five-employee Radical Biology puts out a news release that its new genetically derived painkiller, which it compares to Advil, killed pain better than a placebo and was found to be safe in its Phase I trial. *Big whoop!* It's not like there are no other mid-strength painkillers on the market, right? And anything in Phase I trials is at least a year or two away from the market, even assuming its Phase II and Phase III trials go well.

But what matters is the market's *perception* of the news, and right now you know that the market is going gaga over anything that sounds like it has something to do with applied genetics. So RADB goes on a crazy run, gaining 45 percent in a day and a half.

You know that this is not going to last, and that RADB is not going to hold this level. How could it? This product is not going to advance the frontiers of medicine, and it's doubtful that this tiny company has got a lot more products in the pipeline, so things are almost certainly going to quiet down until some Phase II news comes out. So on the second day you wait for what you believe will be the stock's final push upward, short it near the top, set stops (of course!), and wait for RADB to come tumbling down like Jack and Jill on the steep slope.

Stocks like RADB that run on news can be played during both parts of their journey—long on the way up, and short on the way down. They're ideal for trading because, once you've watched a few, you'll get an idea of just how far traders are willing to push them up and when they'll start to run out of steam. And it's mainly individual traders pushing them up—there probably aren't many real investors who actually buy into these little puppies during an episode like a news run, and the stocks are so cheap and have such low floats that lots of volume can be generated by relatively few trades (compared to large companies with higher-priced shares and huge floats).

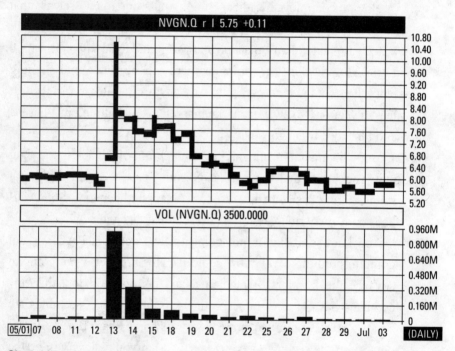

Shortable runup on news. After running up over 80 percent on news that it had reported preliminary evidence that its experimental drug blocked an enzyme that promotes cancer growth, NVGN steadily declined over the following weeks until its share price was actually lower than it had been before the news.
Chart provided by TradePortal.com, Inc.

Hot Sectors/Sympathy Plays

Now that we're on the subject of hot sectors (see also Chapter 4), let's look at a related trend: sympathy plays. When a stock in a hot sector has good news and begins to move up, the stocks of the other companies in the same sector will often start to run up as well—*in sympathy* with the original mover. Likewise, when a stock has bad news and begins to tank, others in the sector will often start to trend down as well. What's the market's rationale behind this? Wouldn't you think that good news for one company would be bad news for its competitors and drive their prices down instead of up?

Well—*no*. As long as the news reflects well on the prospects of the industry or business the newsmaking company is in, a sense of *possibility* is generated in the minds of market players. If one company in the sector is doing well, it's *possible* that demand for the whole sector's business is growing or that the whole sector will develop its products or market so that all the companies in the sector will become powerhouses with stocks as amazing as Microsoft. It's *possible*, isn't it? Yes, it's *possible*. The sector has *potential*.

And that's all the market needs to hear.

A great way to handle sympathy plays is to look at all the stocks in the sector to see whether others have started running with the newsmaker. If so, look for laggards—stocks that should also start running but haven't yet. By buying a laggard, you'll get in at a good price and the stock will have most or all of its run left. Make sure there's no other factor keeping that particular stock from running, such as bad news of its own that will keep it from following the sympathy trend—remember, *news trumps other trends*.

Sectors go through hot and cold phases. Knowing which sectors are hot is especially useful in uncertain markets. Whenever there's a sudden general market rally, only the stocks in the hottest sectors will participate in the rally. Stocks in cold or dying sectors will just sit there, motionless, like ugly little toadstools. Always be aware of which sectors are hot or "in play" so that you're ready to hop into the right stocks when the market rallies. At the same time, be aware of which stocks are wildly overvalued so you'll know what to sell short when the market makes a downturn. As a trader, your goal is to be positioned in the strongest stocks and sectors when you go long, and in the weakest when you go short.

Other Tradable Trends

There are so many trends of all kinds that I can't even begin to discuss them all here. You may discover some new ones yourself. Not all will occur all the time; instead, they operate for a while, then become dormant, then reappear months later. Here's a brief list of some other prominent trends to look for. Remember that *no* trade is a guaranteed sure thing, and that you must *always* use protective and trailing stops on your trades.

For a discussion of the NASDAQ morning gap trend, see Chapter 3.

IPO spinoffs

When the IPO market is booming, this trend is just freakin' awesome. It's also the first trend I discovered.

A company that's going to spin off a part of itself as an IPO tends to move steadily up in price until the IPO date, starting a week or two before that date. On the day the IPO starts to trade—sometimes literally within a minute of the time it hits the market, and sometimes with a brief delay or even a last small price runup—the parent company's stock just up and dies. *Tankola time!* The strategy is to buy the parent once it starts moving in anticipation of the spinoff, sell it the day before the IPO is to begin trading, and then short the parent just *after* the IPO starts to trade. *Double ka-chingo!*

Quiet period expirations

The "quiet period" for IPOs is the twenty-five days after a company goes public. During this time, the SEC forbids the company and the IPO's underwriters to say anything that isn't covered in the company's prospectus or final registration statement. The underwriters face further restrictions on issuing research.

As stocks near the ends of their quiet periods, they tend to steadily rise in price in anticipation of the "strong buy" recommendations most will receive from their underwriters immediately after the quiet period ends. The runup usually begins about ten days prior to the quiet period expiration, and is often accompanied by steadily increasing volume. It's wise to sell quiet period stocks the day before the recommendations will come out.

Why not hold the stock after it gets a "strong buy" recommendation? It's just another case of buy the rumor, sell the news. Another tip: It's best to trade this trend with stocks that have highly respected underwriters and are in hot sectors.

IPO lockup expirations

Another solid trend play is to short stocks with upcoming IPO lockup expirations. An IPO lockup is a period of time, usually from six to eighteen months, when insiders who obtained the IPO at the offering price or less cannot sell their shares. Once this time period has elapsed, insiders often take their money and run. I know I would!

This trend is shortable because the greater the number of shares unlocked, the more likely it is that insiders will start to dump their shares, particularly if the market is not doing well but the share price is still higher than the IPO offering price. (The more shares freed, the better the chance of a negative effect on the share price.) This play works best when the number of shares being unlocked is more than 25 percent of the current float. You should short the stock roughly ten days before the IPO lockup expiration date, since anticipation of the event usually scares traders out of the stock well before its actual date. Cover the short about five days after the expiration date. By that time, most insiders will seem to have sold, and the news will be priced into the stock.

Like any other play, this one is not foolproof—often one of the underwriters will magically upgrade the stock as the lockup expiration approaches, or the company will release news to pump the stock price up to counteract the selling. And be sure to check company news closely, since if the market is bad and share prices are down, lockup periods may be extended.

Index additions

Mutual funds that track major stock indexes *have* to buy any new stock added to an index in order to keep pace and follow its investment guidelines. The larger the market capitalization of the company added to the index, the more shares the funds need to buy. The increased buying pressure on stocks added to indexes tends to drive their prices up, and this trend creates a great trading opportunity.

The stock may or may not begin to move on the day the index addition is announced, but it generally starts to move up in earnest one to two weeks before the addition actually takes place. Once the stock enters the index, its price tends to fall as traders take profits—as they sell the news. It can fall for several days after it's been added to the index. Therefore, this trend can be played long on the way up, until the day the stock is added to the index, and short on the way down, once it's been added.

Window dressing

At the end of each quarter, mutual funds try to dress up their portfolios by buying the stocks that have had the best performance during that quarter. They do this to mislead potential investors into thinking that the fund's managers are great stock pickers. For example, if semiconductor stocks did well during the quarter, funds may load up on them during the last week of the quarter so their "holdings" list will give the impression that they have a clue what they're doing. It's completely superficial, and that's why it's called "window dressing."

It's possible to make money on this trend by buying shares of high-performing stocks just before the end of the quarter to catch the price rise when funds start buying large quantities of them.

The flip side of window dressing is that funds often dump their dog stocks—stocks in any group that's underperformed during the quarter—right before the quarter ends. You can try picking up stocks in underperforming sectors at the end of the quarter, because they'll often be picked up again during the next quarter by the same funds that just dumped them. The funds still want the stock, but they don't want to reveal to investors that they owned so many underachievers.

How to Trade IPOs

When the IPO market is hot, a lot of people get carried away with lust for hot, sexy, must-have IPOs. This makes them commit a trading sin that's much like placing an overnight market order: They place market orders for an IPO before it starts trading on its first day, which leads to outrageous runups in price right when trading opens. For the market maker, these market orders are nothing more than a license to steal. For the trader, they're a sure way to lose money: Your order will be filled at a ridiculously high price that the stock may never see again.

Other traders, who are smart enough not to place orders before trading starts (note that most IPOs start to trade between noon and 1:30 P.M. Eastern), may make a different mistake: They may chase the stock up as it rises in price after trading opens. *Never chase a stock; wait for it to come to you.* Chasing is a great way to be the last one in before the price starts to drop back down to the level you *should* have paid.

RULES OF THE GAME   Don't chase a stock; wait for it to come to you. *Last one in the pool swims with the turd!*

If you're going to try to trade an IPO on its first day, don't place a preopening market order (*duh!*), and don't use market orders *at all*. The way to buy is with a limit order after the stock's price has pulled back a bit and is about to bounce and continue upward again. It's very hard to see where the bounce will take place unless you have Level II, so I don't recommend trading first-day IPOs without that information. The goal is to buy at the bottom, at the bounce level, hold as the price rises, and sell just as the price is about to fall again. You may be able to do this several times, until the stock's momentum drops to the point where it's not making big moves up any more. (You can't short an IPO during its first thirty days on the market.)

If you want to hold the IPO past its first day, it's hard to know exactly when to jump in, but definitely wait until after the initial volatility has ended (it can last up to fifteen minutes). The higher the IPO has opened, the less chance it has of continuing to climb throughout the rest of the day. If the IPO has opened at an outrageously high price, it will probably sink to a fairly stable level in an hour or two. If not, and you think the price could go higher, you might want to buy fairly soon after the initial volatility has ended. One option is to buy half your shares then and wait to see whether there's a slump in the price later in the afternoon when you can buy the rest for less.

Exercises

Evaluating the risk-to-reward ratio for trend plays

Below are four trend plays, each with three possible stocks to play. Which is the best trend trading candidate? Which is the worst?

I. Earnings

Which of the following is the best earnings play? Which is the worst?

Stock A has always had solid earnings. It is expected to beat estimates. Its sector is not particularly hot. The market is mixed.

Stock B has never had any earnings. Its losses are expected to be less than analysts' estimates, meaning that it will beat estimates. Its sector is beyond red-hot—it's white-hot. Other stocks in its sector have run up magnificently during this earnings season. The market is bullish.

Stock C gave an earnings warning weeks ago. Its sector has been hot in the past but isn't now. The market is bullish.

II. Splits

Which of the following is the best splits play? Which is the worst?

Stock A is splitting 2:3. It's in a cold sector. The market is bullish. Lately, the split trend has been weak but visible.

Stock B is splitting 5:1. It's a leader in its sector. It's not in the hottest sector, but the sector is fairly popular. The market is bullish. Lately, the split trend has been weak but visible.

Stock C is splitting 2:1. It's in a relatively hot sector. The market is bearish. Lately, the split trend has been weak but visible.

III. News

Which of the following is the best news play? Which is the worst?

Stock A is a teeny tiny stock in a hot sector. It comes out with a press release announcing a partnership with a larger company. The market is nothing but a cave full of grouchy bears.

Stock B is a strong stock in a cold sector. It comes out with amazing news that suggests incredible future growth. The market is bearish.

Stock C is a strong stock in a hot sector. It comes out with mildly interesting news. The market is a virtual stampede—who let the bulls out?

IV. Hot sectors/sympathy

Which of the following is the best sympathy play? Which is the worst?

Stock A is in a mildly hot sector whose leader has just announced huge growth in sales and has moved up on the news. Stock A hasn't moved on the news. The market is mixed.

Stock B is in a very hot sector whose leader has just announced huge growth in sales and has moved up on the news. Stock B has jumped 20 percent on the news. The market is bullish.

Stock C is in a hot sector whose leader has just announced a fairly routine partnership with another company. The market is bullish.

V. Discussion

I. Earnings: Stock B is the best, and Stock C is the worst. Being in a hot sector in a bull market makes up for a multitude of sins. Since Stock B has never had any earnings, it is full of golden *potential*—there's no way to calculate how enormous its earnings possibilities might be. Stock C, having given a warning, is not a candidate for an earnings run at all.

II. Splits: Stock B is the best, and Stock A is the worst. Stock B, with a whopping 5:1 split, is a good company in a solid sector, and a bullish market makes the splits trend more likely to work. If any stock will revive the trend, it's a solid company with a 5:1 split. Stock A is hardly worth looking at as a split candidate because its ratio is a weak 2:3. Even though the market is bullish, Stock A's cold sector will keep it from reviving the trend.

III. News: Stock C is the best, and Stock A is the worst. The bullish market will make any good news travel further, even if, like Stock C's, it's only mildly interesting. Stock A is worse than Stock B because a bear market will ignore less-than-impressive news about a small company, while fantastic news about a good company could actually spark a rally.

IV. Hot sectors/sympathy: Stock A is the best, and Stock B is the worst. Stock A is in a great position to run but hasn't started yet, so as a laggard, it's ripe for the picking. Stock B would have been a good play if you'd gotten to it sooner, but the risk-to-reward ratio isn't favorable now because all the reward may already be gone.

Chapter 7

Hot Tips from Hell

Five Bad Ways to Pick Stocks

Recognize When You're Out of Ideas

A lot of traders get themselves into trouble when they feel the itch to trade but have no idea what to buy. Like gamblers in a casino, they crave the *action*. So they go out trolling for ideas, surfing the Web in search of inspiration. They forget that they should *never* buy a stock unless they have *a good, sound reason and a plan*. Without a good reason, buying a stock is no better than putting money on the roulette table, and sometimes much worse.

RULES OF THE GAME   Always have a reason. No reason, no play!

Stock Tips Are for Losers

Why mince words? *Stock tips are for losers!*

This is a good general rule to follow. Sure, sometimes a random stock tip will pan out, but it's also true that even a broken clock is right twice a day! There are lots of ways to pick stocks, and some make *way* more sense than others. A method is great if it works out more than 40 percent of the time. A method is not so great if it works out less often than that. But there are a few ways to pick stocks that are virtually guaranteed to *lose* you money at least 90 percent of the time. (If you're *trying* to lose money, I suggest that you either spend it on therapy instead or find a better tax accountant.) Most of these losing methods are various forms of stock tips.

For those who understand why it's good to know which stock-picking methods suck the worst, I'll list them for you here. Some of them may seem way beyond obvious, but it can be amazingly easy to give in to temptation when you're vulnerable—even when you know better. You'd never believe how many smart people lose money in these ways every single day of the market.

RULES OF THE GAME   Most tips don't pan out.

WAXIE'S STREET SMARTS

A good stock picker like Waxie may give out suggestions for trades that he is making in his own account. This is not the kind of losing stock tip discussed in this chapter. A good, well-reasoned suggestion that you can check out yourself is completely different from someone telling you to buy a stock "because it's definitely going to go up." Waxie always tells members of his chat room at Trend-Fund.com that they should never blindly follow his picks, but should consider each one carefully and make informed decisions.

Five Absurdly Bad Ways to Pick Stocks

Here is my list of the top five boneheaded ways to find stocks to buy. I can say this because I've committed many of these trading sins myself, lost money, learned from my mistakes, and come to care deeply about helping everyone else avoid learning the hard way.

1. Idle chat by the hopeful and naive:

Wishful thinking presented as fact on Internet bulletin boards by well-meaning but hopelessly ignorant and biased investors.

2. Manipulation by touts and pump-and-dumpers:

Bulletin board posts and e-mails from real fraudsters and con artists.

3. Paid stock promoters:

Web sites containing stock "analysis" that looks unbiased but isn't because the "analyst" has a personal financial interest.

4. OTC/BB stock recommendations:

Tips on garbage-can stocks that are guaranteed losers. If anyone recommends an OTC/BB stock to you, you should never listen to them again.

5. Wall Street professionals' recommendations:

Hype by investment banks, analysts, and brokers, including those on TV.

Let's see what happens to people who try these five losing ways to pick stocks.

Idle Chat by the Hopeful and Naive

You've heard that it's good to be an informed investor, so you read a lot of stuff you find on the Internet. One of the things you like to do is to check out bulletin boards on financial Web sites like Raging Bull and Silicon Investor. You can go to the bulletin board for a specific stock and see what *everyone* has to say about it. A lot of people—mostly people who own the stock—will write posts saying it's the next Microsoft, better than Cisco at its peak, or guaranteed to double in six months.

The traps here are sunny, well-meaning optimism and its dark twin, anxious hope. People have bought a stock, and they want it to do well. They really believe that it will do well. At least, they *really hope* it will do well. And they love to talk about it! They'll tell you how great the company is, how sharp the management, how incredible the business plan. They'll tell you the stock will go up 50 percent by the end of the year. They have inside information, which they're generous enough to share with the bulletin board. They know people who work at the company. They work at a company that buys stuff from it. They know all kinds of stuff, and they have opinions! The stock is a winner, a champ, a gem in the rough. It's the next big thing, or it's a powerhouse that will never slow down. It makes you feel good just to be associated with this stock! It confers power and sex appeal. And it will make you rich!

Other times, people (out of the goodness of their hearts, always) will offer you a hot tip—just because they want to be nice. They may sincerely believe in their tip, and they may have put a lot of their own money into the stock they're hyping. But none of that makes it a good play.

The trouble is, these people really don't know anything, and they're the opposite of objective. They've fallen in love with their stocks and their tips, and they can't gauge the risk accurately and weigh it against a realistic sense of the possible reward. All they can see is the reward, and it seems unlimited in size.

So, you're cleverly thinking, if these ignorant, biased stockholders don't know anything, maybe I should do exactly the *opposite* of whatever they say. If they say buy, maybe I should sell short. If they say sell, I should buy.

The problem with this idea is that trying to decide what to do based on sheer nonsense doesn't make any better sense. These people's opinions aren't the polar opposite of the truth, they just *don't mean anything*—they're totally irrelevant. It's like deciding which direction to go by flipping a coin and then going in the direction opposite to how the flip turned out. It may be right and it may be wrong, but the right answer has nothing to do with the coin flip. And these investors could be right just as easily as they're wrong—they're just completely random. I'll say it again: Even a broken clock is right twice a day!

You'll also see comments on electronic bulletin boards that say things like, "This stock sucks. The company reeks of mismanagement. You're all going to lose your shirts." These posts are written by short sellers, also unobjective, who are trying to scare everyone into selling their stock so the price goes down and the shorter can cover at a nice profit.

This is not to say that message boards have no utility at all. They can provide some useful information. Say a stock suddenly goes up and you have no idea why. There's no news on the company, it's not following the market, and nothing else explains the price rise. This is a good time to check the message boards—not because they'll give you the truth (and remember, the Truth is irrelevant in the market anyway), but because they might tell you what it is that's driving other traders to buy. It may be a rumor, or it may be something else you've somehow missed. If it's some sort of verifiable news, of course you have to check it out yourself by consulting a reliable source such as TrendFund.com. After it's verified, you'll decide what it means in terms of your trading decision—is it important enough, the right time, etc.? (See Chapter 6 on how to pick stocks using tools such as news.) You can then make an informed, intelligent assessment of the probable risk and benefit.

Manipulation by Touts and Pump-and-Dumpers

Would you buy stock based on a cold call? Promise me you never will. Have you seen the movie *Boiler Room*? If not, rent it *now*. (And no, I can only wish I had some personal interest in the film's royalties.)

What goes on in *Boiler Room*, where a bunch of dodgy stockbrokers sit around giving naive, gullible people cold calls and talking them into buying worthless stocks, is *exactly* what goes on on the Internet—except that it's so much easier to e-mail a list of hundreds of people or post a message that thousands will see than it is to call one person at a time on the phone. Plenty of people have been criminally prosecuted for this sort of stock manipulation. Reports of cases regularly show up in the *New York Times* business section. These are known as "pump-and-dump" schemes.

TRADER TALK   A *pump-and-dump* scheme is a fraudulent activity in which touters "pump" up a stock's price by hyping it to investors or by spreading fictitious good news or rumors. Once the price has risen precipitously, the pumpers then "dump" their shares onto the market at a profit and cause the price to crash, never to recover. Unwitting investors who buy at the inflated price lose their money as the price falls.

Paid Stock Promoters

Mr. Loser sees a press release: Analyst Wilbur Kartoffel of Wall Street Partners, Inc. has come out with a Strong Buy rating for FlimsyTech Corporation of Miami, Florida. The press release goes on to tell all about how much growth potential the company has, how good its financials look, and so forth. The release refers readers to a full report on the company at www.wallstreetpartnersinc.com.

The report on the Web site looks thorough and carefully considered. It goes on for five pages and describes in great detail the business plan, the projected earnings, and other enticing corporate characteristics. Mr. Loser does not see the fine print at the very bottom of the last page where it says, "Wall Street Partners, Inc. may have received stock or monetary compensation in exchange for performing this analysis."

So what? you ask. Don't all Wall Street analysts get paid for their work? Well, sure, and while there's nothing good to say even about real Wall Street analysts (the ones at big investment banks), these paid promoters are bad in a different way. They're basically flacks hired by questionable companies that can't attract the attention of regular analysts, and the sole purpose of these paid mouthpieces is to hype the stock to potential investors. They're far less reputable than analysts at investment banks, and you'll see what I think of those regular analysts a little later in this chapter.

Bottom line: Read every stock "analysis" carefully and look for the magic word "compensation" to see whether the writeup was done by a paid promoter instead of a regular Wall Street analyst. If so, ask yourself what kind of company would need to hire someone to tout it.

But wait, you say. It just says that the promoters *may* have gotten compensation. Maybe they weren't actually compensated at all. And even if they were, maybe they agreed to be paid in stock, which means they must think it's worth something.

Those maybes and a dollar will buy you a cheap cup of coffee. Don't be naive: "May have received" means *received*, and "stock or monetary compensation" means *money*. You're being told exactly what's going on, if you're willing to read and understand. The disclaimer might as well have said, "Wall Street Partners, Inc. may have received monetary compensation or a year's worth of used kitty litter in exchange for performing this analysis." Which do you think is more likely? Which is the true value of the stock?

Always avoid stocks touted by paid promoters.

OTC/BB Stocks

Often, stocks promoted by paid promoters are over-the-counter/ bulletin board stocks. Whether they're hyped or not, OTC/BB stocks are an entire group of stocks that should be avoided like the plague, *without exception.*

T R A D E R T A L K ***OTC/BB stocks*** ("over-the-counter/bulletin board" stocks) aren't listed or traded on any exchange. Because they're not subject to the reporting requirements of listed stocks, little or no financial or other information is available about the companies they represent. OTC/BB stocks are also known as ***bulletin board stocks, unlisted stocks, penny stocks***, or ***pink sheet stocks***. (Don't confuse OTC/BB stocks with NASDAQ OTC stocks, which are listed NASDAQ stocks.)

WAXIE'S STREET SMARTS

OTC/BB stocks *suck out loud*! Just about all OTC/BB stocks are issued by companies with *serious* problems. Many are outright frauds or are run by criminals or near-criminals. The Mafia has been known to be involved in OTC/BB pump-and-dump schemes.

If you now think dot-com and other Internet stocks are garbage cans, any OTC/BB stock is a hundred times worse. At least companies traded on the NASDAQ, NYSE, and AMEX have to report financial information on a regular basis and are regulated by their stock exchanges. They at least have to *act* like real companies. OTC/BB companies don't have to reveal *any* information to *anyone*—and they usually don't want to, because a lot of times these companies are nothing but a room with a telephone. You don't believe me? If not, you're being naive.

So now you're saying, But Waxie, who cares if it's a real company if I can make a quick buck on the stock just by trading it? I won't invest in the stock but just trade in and out of it.

Well, this is the deal: First of all, OTC/BB stocks are manipulated by insiders, mob types, and small-time fraudsters *all the time*. These stocks are incredibly easy to move by starting false rumors or artificially creating price movements—and these are criminal activities. So why shouldn't you ride the stock up with the fraudsters, assuming you're doing nothing illegal? Well, first of all, there's the fact that you'd be intentionally contributing to the criminal ruin of all the poor schmoes who got in after you. I'll say a bit more on that below.

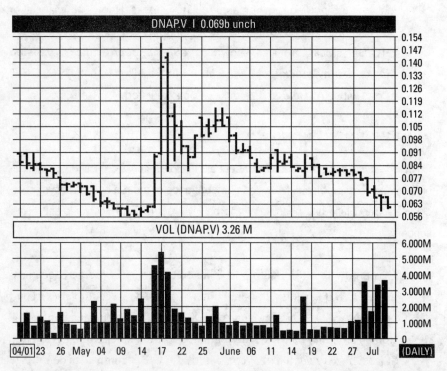

An OTC/BB stock's precipitous rise and fall. On May 16 and 17, DNAP spiked for no apparent reason, lost much of its gain the following day, and then returned to its previous level.
Chart provided by TradePortal.com, Inc.

Besides that, though, you're almost certainly going to get in too late yourself, right at the top, and the stock is going to start going down right after you buy it. These schemes are designed to take advantage of people exactly like you. Pump-and-dump scams are meant to benefit only the people setting them up, not people looking for a free ride—and there's almost no chance that one is going to benefit you.

If that's not enough, there's the little problem of stops: The ugly fact is that *you can't set stops on OTC/BB stocks*. It just isn't possible. The only kind of orders you can use on an OTC/BB stock are market and limit orders, so in terms of limiting your losses, you're at the mercy of the market maker and the market. When the stock tanks, as it almost always does, you won't be the first one in line to get out, and the price will drop *a lot* before you can.

WAXIE'S STREET SMARTS

It's not possible to use stops on OTC/BB stocks! This is reason enough to avoid them *completely*.

Now, back to our moral question: Why should buying into the artificial runup of an OTC/BB stock, knowing it will inevitably tank, be any worse than buying a listed stock when you know it will tank? If you're as cynical about the entire Wall Street game as I am, that's a reasonable question. Here's the answer. I'm not an investor and I don't ever want to be, but at least there are people and institutions who invest in listed companies, and though I don't recommend it, it may not be a completely wacked thing to do in certain market environments. No one with a grain of sense, though, would seriously *invest* in an OTC/BB stock. It's probably actually worse than gambling in a casino, because your money is almost certain to disappear—at the casino, you have at least *some* odds of winning. Still, there are people who lack even a grain of sense and do try to invest in these stocks. They may deserve pity and definitely need enlightenment, but they don't deserve more abuse. Even if I thought I could make money on OTC/BB stocks (which I don't), I wouldn't want to contribute to the misery of ignorant, desperate people.

N E W B I E   T R A P   Lots of newbies are attracted by the "cheapness" of penny stocks because you can buy so many shares for so little. *This is faulty thinking.* What matters is the *percentage* you have to gain, the *likelihood* that you'll gain it, and the *percentage* you can lose. You can lose just as much money on ten thousand shares of a fifty-cent pink sheet stock as you can on fifty shares of a hundred-dollar NASDAQ stock, and it's even more likely that you will. The upside is worse, too, because the chances of actually *making* money on an OTC/BB stock are ridiculously low.

Wall Street Professionals' Recommendations

My opinion of Wall Street suits is pretty simple: All analysts suck! All brokers suck!

WAXIE'S STREET SMARTS
Remember: All analysts suck! All brokers suck! If anything, they're good contrarian indicators.

T R A D E R   T A L K   A *contrarian indicator* is a market indicator that appears to show that the market is headed in a particular market direction, but which a contrarian would take as a sign that the market will head in the opposite direction. For example, when every analyst on TV is saying that the market will never stop going up, this would appear to indicate that the market will keep going up; as a contrarian indicator, though, it suggests that the market will soon go down.

As you read in Chapter 4, the job of Wall Street analysts is to get people to buy stock in companies their firms represent, and the job of brokers is to make as many buy and sell transactions as they can. That's how these people earn their living. It only makes sense that their primary interest is in getting you to buy stock, not in making sure it's a good idea for you. Whether or not it's really a good investment is simply not their concern. If you pay any attention to the way institutional analysts set price targets and upgrade and downgrade stocks, you'll see that it's all a cynical game. And since analysts who appear on TV are expected to say something even if they have no idea what's going on or what's going to happen, they often just say anything, figuring that in a few weeks no one will remember what they've said. Most of them have little understanding of what's going on in the market. So why are they on TV? Well, you could ask the same question about most of what's on TV. It's only there because people watch it, and as long as people watch it, it'll be there.

Lots of people, including me, have lost lots of money listening to analysts and brokers. Learn from their mistakes and don't make the same ones yourself.

Be Skeptical

Take your doubts seriously.

There are lots of other bad ways to pick stocks besides the ones I've talked about, and as a rule of thumb, if something seems like a bad idea, it probably is. Even if you decide against it and it works, ask yourself whether it *should* have worked or whether this time was the exception, the one time in a hundred when this idea worked for no reason other than random chance. Don't take a fluke for granted. Think about it and become a more intelligent trader.

If you hear a little voice inside saying, "I probably shouldn't do this," *listen to it*! Give yourself and your instincts some credit! It's much better to be too cautious than to lose money by taking too many risks. If you find yourself thinking, "*Maybe* it will work" or "I *hope* it will work," *just say no to the whole thing*! "Maybe" and "hope" are dirty words to a good trader, and they're two words I never want to hear.

R U L E S   O F   T H E   G A M E   Don't play maybes. When in doubt, stay out!

Good Picking Is Only Half the Battle

Always remember that even if you pick a good stock for good reasons, you can still lose money if you don't trade it using the sound trading practices discussed in Chapters 8 through 11. Good stock picking is only half the battle. It's *always* possible to lose money on a good pick if you play it badly.

Now it's time to learn how to *play to win*!

Chapter 8

Planning the Trade and Trading the Plan

How to Enter, Maintain, and Exit the Play

This chapter covers:

- Why having a plan for every trade minimizes risk and maximizes reward
- Why finding the right entry point is as important as finding a good stock
- How to enter a stock position
- The 10 A.M. rule
- How to hold positions safely
- Five reasons to close a position
- How to close a position
- Why you must never "marry" a stock

Always Play to Win!

I've heard it said that with each action we take, we are moving either toward death or toward life. In the market, every trade you make is a trade either toward losing or toward winning. And within every trade, each step—entering, holding, and exiting—also moves you toward either winning or losing. That's why each step requires planning, attention, and discipline.

RULES OF THE GAME Play to win!

Plan the Trade and Trade the Plan

Before you take a position in a stock, *you must always have a plan*. People have different styles—for example, some take profits in a staggered fashion and others close trades all at once—but whatever yours is, you must know what your plan is *before you buy the stock*. The most successful traders *always* have a plan, and they *always* stick to it unless there's an unusual and compelling reason not to, such as a change in market conditions.

RULES OF THE GAME Plan the trade and trade the plan.

Why is this so important? First of all, having a plan means you've thought about why you're making the trade in the first place—you have *a compelling reason* for the trade and you see that it has *a good risk-to-reward ratio*. Without a reason for the trade and a sense of what the reward should be, there's no way you can form a rational plan. ("I'll hold it and see what happens" is not a plan. That's gambling. So is relying on luck.) Second, having a plan eliminates the "deer caught in the headlights" reaction that it's natural to have when a stock you bought starts to move in the wrong direction. That paralysis can be fatal. If you have a plan, you know exactly what to do and when you need to do it. You'll have thought out the possible outcomes ahead of time. There's nothing to panic about. Third, besides minimizing the risk of panic, having a plan also minimizes other kinds of risk and maximizes reward because, by following the plan, you force yourself to act only in advantageous ways. You'll minimize risk and maximize reward by choosing a profitable entry point (and avoiding money-losing entries), holding your position safely (keeping stops set where you've planned to set them), and exiting profitably at an appropriate time.

How can you know where the right entry and exit points are? You can't know, unless you're psychic, but that doesn't matter because *trading isn't about knowing things for certain. Instead, it's about gauging probabilities.* If you always do the things that have the highest probability of working, they should work out many more times than not. And that's what trading is all about.

How to Enter a Position

Finding a low-risk entry point for a trade is every bit as important as finding a good stock. How can this be? Think about it for a few seconds and you'll realize that you can pick the best stock in the world, but if you enter it at the wrong place, you may make no profit on it at all—and you may actually lose money. Some foolish investment "gurus" in recent years have been preaching the dangerous sermon that it doesn't matter when a long-term investor buys a stock, or at what price. The thinking (if you can call it that) is that if the stock is a good stock, you'll make money on it after enough time has passed, and any price fluctuations that occur now will look like tiny hiccups when it's made you rich many years hence. All I have to say about that is that the people who bought stocks like Celera Genomics at nearly $250 a share and still held it at $40 a share a year later probably could have done much better things with their money than buy a hyped-up stock at its very peak.

Nobody knows which stocks are going to stay the course and make them rich in five or ten years. *Many companies won't even be around in five or ten years.* Doesn't it make sense for anyone, trader or investor, to enter a stock at a point where it has a better chance of actually making them money instead of losing them so much that they have to wait five years just to get their initial investment back?

All right, then: Where is a safe entry point, and how do you make sure you enter there?

Finding a sensible entry point involves knowing the time frame of your trade (for a particular trend play, for example, you might know that you should enter no earlier than a week before the event creating the trend); looking at charts to see where the stock has been and where its support and resistance levels are (and thinking about psychological support and resistance levels); and waiting for a pullback in price if you believe that the price is temporarily high and that it will drop and create a better buying opportunity for you.

The way to make sure you enter where you plan to is to *use a limit order*. Limit orders sometimes make you wait behind others who placed their orders at the same price before you did, but in most situations, placing a reasonable limit order is the only sane way to enter a position. *Always use limit orders*—with only the rarest exceptions. *Market orders should be used only in the most extreme emergencies.*

TRADER TALK   A *limit order* is an order that can execute only at the stated price or better. Check with your broker; some brokers use slightly different names for various order types.

....
WAXIE'S STREET SMARTS
With extremely few exceptions, *use only limit orders.*

In certain situations, it may make sense to stagger your entry by buying half the shares you want at a price you think may be the lowest the stock will reach, and then waiting to buy the other half either when the price does get better ("averaging down") or when the stock starts to move ("adding on strength").

The *wrong* way to enter a position is to chase a moving stock. Chasing stocks is a form of panic, and it practically guarantees that you'll pay too much for the stock. Why is it so bad to pay too much? The more you pay for a stock, the further your risk-to-reward ratio is shifted away from reward (because your upside is decreased) and toward risk (because the probability of the run ending increases as the stock gets more and more expensive). There are two ways to look at the decrease in your upside: First of all, you'll capture less of the stock's movement, so your percentage return will be less; second, the more the stock costs per share, the fewer shares you'll be able to buy, and any return you get will be multiplied by fewer shares. So your entry price matters a lot.

RULES OF THE GAME Don't chase a stock; wait for it to come to you. *Last one in the pool swims with the turd!*

Remember, it doesn't matter if you miss a play. *It is not the last good stock!* There will *always* be more stocks to play. It's much better to sit one out than to chase it and end up with a loss.

Morning gaps down present good opportunities to buy stocks you want. *Buying a gap down* is a good way to enter a position. This is because *when a stock gaps down, it often opens near what will turn out to be the low of the day*. On the other hand, *buying a gap up* is one of the *worst* trades you can make. This is because the gap up generally reflects the market's level of interest in the stock. Any good news from overnight has often already been priced in. For that reason, the stock's opening price and volatility on a gap up often also turn out to establish the stock's high of the day. Therefore, buying (really chasing) the gap up means that you are very likely buying the stock for top dollar. *A good trader buys stocks that still have upside that's not yet priced into the stock.*

Likewise, entering a short position on a gap up is a great plan, and shorting a gap down is hopelessly foolish. The opening price and volatility on a gap down often turn out to establish the stock's low of the day, so shorting at the lowest point is a useless and risky activity.

What do you do if you want to buy a stock but the market gaps up instead of down? What if you want to short but the market gaps down? If this happens, the plan is to let your trading be guided by the "10 A.M. rule."

The 10 A.M. Rule

The 10 A.M. rule is a simple rule that will save you *bags* of money over the long haul. What is it?

Let's say you want to buy a stock, for whatever reason—a trend play, a market rally that you think a currently hot sector will participate in, or whatever. You know that a great time to buy would be on a gap down, but the market is in rally mode and instead of gapping down, the stock gaps up. You know that buying the gap up is way beyond stupid, so what can you do?

Using the 10 A.M. rule, *you wait until after 10 A.M.* to buy your stock. If the stock makes a *new* high for the day sometime after 10 A.M., then and *only* then can you play the stock, using stops to protect yourself.

Anyone who's followed the market for a while knows that the market will often gap up, only to suddenly sell off and reverse into negative territory. By following the 10 A.M. rule, you avoid the risk of a sudden reversal. If the stock makes a new high after 10 A.M., it means that there is still trader interest in the stock, so it stands a good chance of gaining momentum and heading higher.

Along these lines, it's a good idea to watch for a hot sector in the morning and follow the stocks in the sector that are up for the day. If they are still making new highs at midday, they stand a good chance of finishing the day near their ultimate highs for the day.

Here is an example of the 10 A.M. rule on a gap up:

- ZEST closes at $145

- After hours, ZEST announces a two-for-one stock split

- The next morning ZEST gaps up to open at $161

- ZEST trades as high as $166 before 10 A.M.

- For two hours it trades lower and doesn't see $166 again

- At 2 P.M., ZEST hits $166.50

- ZEST is now buyable, using the 10 A.M. rule

- Had ZEST never made it over $166 after 10 A.M., you probably should not have bought it

The 10 A.M. rule also applies in a down market and to stocks that gap down (open at prices lower than where they closed the previous day). In that situation, you should not short a stock that has gapped down unless and until it makes a new low for the day after 10 A.M.

How to Hold a Position

The next part of your plan involves keeping your position out of trouble while you hold it and wait for the ka-chingos. The most important part of this step involves *setting stops*. You must set stops on every trade. This topic is so important that all of Chapter 9 is devoted to it.

RULES OF THE GAME   Always use stops.

When making your plan, you must decide whether, if the trade goes against you, you want to stop out of the stock at a small loss and abandon the trade or average down by increasing your holdings at a lower price, keeping a looser stop in place even farther down. In most cases, the best idea is to stop out at a small loss. There aren't many times when averaging down is a good idea. You should limit it to extremely low-risk plays with high chances of success, in which you've determined that a price decrease to the level where you'd average down is not a sign of impending tankage but just an unexciting temporary move in a range. The best way to figure this out is by looking at support levels on charts. You should also *want* to own more of the stock.

Averaging down does not mean you don't have to set stops. It just means you'll set them lower and give the stock more room to move around before you pull the plug on it.

How to Close a Position

Now that you've started to rack up some ka-chingos on your trade, your plan should tell you when it's time to say good-bye. Knowing when to exit is extremely important, because people who hold on too long often find that their paper profits have disappeared and they've ended up making no money—or even incurring a loss—on what should have been an excellent trade. This should *never* happen to you.

It's useful to think about how the risk-to-reward ratio changes as a stock you're holding long rises in price. It's easy to see that the reward left to gain decreases as the profits in your portfolio increase; there's less there because you've already collected most of it. The risk rises as well. As the price rises to a point where traders start to question how much more it can move, they will start to take profits. As they do, the selling pressure will increase and the stock will edge closer and closer to Tank City. That's why the risk increases as the potential reward decreases. And if the risk is increasing while the reward decreases, at some point your risk-to-reward ratio will become unfavorable. That point is something you should have figured out, as part of your plan, before you bought the stock. Your plan may specify a particular number you've chosen as the exit point, or it may tell you to exit when the volume dries up, or to use trailing stops and hold the stock until a trailing stop is triggered. All of these are firm plans that tell you when to leave the position. Your exit plan also may have alternative exit points, and may tell you that if any of several possible things happen, you should exit.

Target Prices Are Only a Planning Tool

When you first form your plan for a trade, you should consider approximately what price or price range you think the stock is likely to reach. You can call this a target price, but this label gives some traders the wrong impression of its purpose.

A target price is not a price that the stock has to meet. A stock does not *have* to do anything, and certainly not just because you think it will or you want it to. If you treat your target price as a goal, it can lead to all sorts of trouble and false expectations.

Instead, your target price should be used as a planning tool.

The target price helps you figure out your risk-to-reward ratio. It also gives you an exit point, or at least a point where you'll reassess whether you believe the stock can continue to move upward. Your stock may never reach your target price, though. Other things can interfere with its progress. And there's always the possibility that you set your target higher than you should have.

Since there's no way all your plays will hit your price targets, it can be a good idea to make a habit of selling half your shares at a more conservative target. Routinely taking profits along the way will reward you in the long run. Don't get greedy. Remember, pigs get slaughtered!

RULES OF THE GAME Greed = Death. *Pigs get slaughtered!*

There are a number of things that can interfere with the progress of a stock's movement and force you to bail out sooner than you'd anticipated. What to do if any of these possibilities become realities should all be part of your plan. Along these lines, there are *five reasons you should always close a position*, whether or not it has made it to the price you thought it would:

1. The end of a trend

You realize the trend isn't working anymore.

2. Broken momentum

The stock's upward movement has fizzled out or been abruptly broken.

3. An approaching major psychological barrier

The stock is about to reach $100 or $200 a share (you probably should have anticipated this as part of your plan).

4. An approaching technical barrier

The stock is about to reach a resistance level it's been unable to break through before (again, you should have anticipated this as part of your plan).

5. Unsafe market conditions

A sudden marketwide tank-o-rama, the threat of one, or serious uncertainty.

Bailing out of a trade is not a big deal. Quite the contrary—it's good trading. The best traders would rather lose a small profit than take an unnecessary risk. You don't have to win on every trade; no one does, and it's dangerous to try. It can lead to huge mistakes, like marrying stocks. In fact, by limiting losses, a good trader can be profitable overall by making money on only 40 percent of his trades.

RULES OF THE GAME   You don't need to win on every trade.

Stick to Your Plan, and Never Marry a Stock!

A plan is useful only if you follow it. One of the most effective ways to enforce a plan is to use stop-loss orders (see Chapter 9).

By contrast, one of the worst consequences of straying from a plan is marrying a stock.

Why shouldn't you hold a stock long term to wait for it to be profitable?

All the time, people say that they like or even *love* a stock, and that they *know* the stock will always go up in the end. *Right, uh-huh, sure it will!* Even if it eventually did, the whole time these lovers were busy holding on to their stock for dear life and praying for it to go up (even though the market was in the midst of a correction), better traders were shorting it and watching it go down. Or else they were off trading something else that probably made them ten times what those lovers will ever realize on the love stock they've married.

RULES OF THE GAME   Don't marry stocks.

Stocks are not human, and they aren't worthy of love. Let me tell you how I see it. I've been told I'm a very lovin' kinda guy. But I'll tell you what—I don't just throw my love around, or even my *like*. I don't believe in unconditional love in most cases—I have to be loved back as well. Using this as a model, if I own a stock that keeps going down, my love is not being reciprocated, is it? Sorry, that don't work for me! Call me fickle, but I only love a stock when I own it and it's going up. As soon as it shows me signs it wants to go to tanksville, I say good-bye and move on to the next stock.

Remember, when the market corrects itself, which it always does, *no stock is immune*, no matter how much you love it. I've seen many investors watch as their stocks' values were cut in half or more, yet still they held, not wanting to be left out of a big gain—or so deep in loss that they felt they couldn't possibly sell now.

Even if you believe that all stocks will recover from their losses (and the truth is that not all of them will), this is a terrible way to trade. You tie up too much capital, and your rate of return plummets. The better approach is this: You can own them, just don't marry them!

Just as you shouldn't marry stocks, you also should never marry ideas. By this I mean becoming so fond of a particular strategy or trend that you cling to it even after it's stopped working. That's basically the same mistake as marrying a stock—being so sure that it will eventually, finally work that you stay there even after the signs are unmistakable that *it's not going to work out*. Just bag it and start fresh with something else. You'll be happier, and you'll make much more money.

Chapter 9

Hard Hat Zone

Setting Stops on Every Trade

This chapter covers:

- Why you must limit risk and protect profits by using stop-loss orders ("stops") on *every* trade
- What will happen if you don't use stops
- How to set stops
- How to use market conditions, stock-specific factors, and context to decide how tightly to set stops
- How much loss you should tolerate on any trade
- How to use trailing stops to protect profits
- How to recover from a bad loss

TRADER TALK A *stop* is an order you can place with your broker to sell a stock you own if it *drops* to a specified price. It's called a stop because it *stops* you from losing any more money on the position. If you've sold short, you can place a stop order to buy to cover if the stock *rises* to a specified price.

The Market Is a Hard-Hat Zone

Get into the habit of thinking of the market as a construction site. It's a work in progress that goes through many different phases, and lots of unexpected things happen there. Sometimes things that looked perfectly stable in the morning fall down in the afternoon. Things that looked solid suddenly come loose and slide to the ground. In fact, you can *count* on "accidents" happening at regular intervals. Every so often there's bound to be one; the only thing you don't know is when or how the accident will come.

Just as you must wear a hard hat while working in a construction zone—unless you're a half-wit or suicidal!—you *must* protect yourself when you work in the market. As a trader, your protection is the stop-loss order, or "stop."

There Are No Guarantees in the Market

Without protection, the stock market is not a safe place for your money. Forget anything you've heard to the contrary.

During bull markets and early in bear markets, many people find it incredibly hard to understand that the market will not keep their money safe. They believe that, no matter what, the market and "good stocks" will "always come back," as though this were a law of nature.

There's no such law of nature. *Stocks don't always come back. The market doesn't always come back.* If you think about it a little, you should start to ask yourself things like this: "Why *should* a stock continue to go up forever? Does *anything* in this world go on *forever*? Can a company's value reach infinity?" If you want to think about the market in terms of laws of nature, the best one to have in mind is the law of gravity: "What goes up must come down." This is especially true for stocks and sectors that have risen extremely fast, beyond any rational relation to value.

The Horror, Part I: True Stories of Market Disaster

Falling stock prices can wipe out your capital so fast you won't know what hit you. Here are just two examples of what can happen when you least expect it, and how things actually can be worse—*much* worse—than you ever imagined.

Consider the following charts based upon actual market events during March and April 2000 (this was even before the bear market *truly* took hold).

■ Celera Genomics (CRA) dropped 70 percent in only four weeks, helped by a statement by Bill Clinton and Tony Blair on March 14, 2000, favoring free access to human genome sequences and calling on genomics researchers to make their data freely available. Celera's business plan was to make money through patents on its genomics databases.

Think that's bad?

■ Microstrategy Inc. (MSTR) dropped 60 percent *in only one day* after announcing that its quarterly results wouldn't meet analysts' estimates. Changed accounting methods (read: *accurate* account-ing) had forced it to restate revenues and operating results. (The same day, it changed its 1999 full-year results from a profit of 15 cents per share to a loss of up to 51 cents per share—*quite* a differ-ent story.)

Such volatility is common in today's markets. That's pretty obvi-ous, and everybody *knows* it, but they all seem to think it won't affect *their* stocks. This is the kind of thinking that leads people to buy a bunch of stock on margin and then lose their entire investment (and probably owe their broker a little above that, as a kicker) when everything suddenly turns south.

And sudden crashes aren't the only kind of stock market disaster. There's also the horror of a slow, grinding ride down over a period of weeks and months. Look at the chart for just about any technology or dot-com stock between spring 2000 and spring 2001 and you'll see losses of 50 percent, 75 percent, even 90 percent. Some charts *won't even be available* because the companies have gone out of business. Let me list just a few that are extinct: EToys.com, Pets.com, Mother-Nature.com, Garden.com, WebVan. Dozens of companies, including some that were real hotties in their glory days, have been delisted. The only people who'll remember these stocks in a few years are the ones who *lost their entire investment* or much of it because they never knew when to get out. They didn't have a plan to bail at a certain point by limiting their losses.

They didn't set stops.

The Horror, Part II: Losing on a Winning Trade

Losing the money you put into a trade isn't the only kind of disaster stops can stop. There's another one: making a great trade, running up a nice paper profit, and then watching it slip away until you *actually start to lose money* on the trade. Think this can never happen to you? If you don't use stops, it can and it will.

A classic Mr. Loser adventure will illustrate this particular horror show. Mr. Loser buys a boatload of Orbit Galactic Corp. for $10,000 and watches the little rocket ship double in price in only three days. He's made $10,000 in three days, and he's ecstatic! The stock then weakens and falls a little, but he doesn't want to sell it yet. He thinks, *What if it turns around and goes up another 50 percent? That would be worth another $5,000. It would* suck *to miss out on that profit!* So he keeps holding Orbit, *hoping* (how I hate that word!) that it will recover and continue to the moon. He holds and it drops, and he thinks about how much he wants his profit back, and he holds some more and it drops and drops some more, and he finally ends up losing money on what had been a very profitable trade. This should *never* happen to a trader, but it actually happens *all the time.*

What was Mr. Loser's mistake?

He didn't protect his profits with trailing stops.

Both of these unspeakable horrors—losing your capital and losing your profits—are completely avoidable if you protect yourself with stops.

What Is a Stop?

Stops are not complicated. When I use the word "stop," I'm referring to a *stop-loss order*. This is an order that directs your broker to sell a stock you hold long if it *drops* to a specified price. If you've sold short, you can place a stop-loss buy-to-cover order to get out of the position if the stock *rises to* a specified price. Once the stop is triggered, it's immediately executed as a market order.

Here's an example. Let's say you buy TechniDaydream, Inc. at $50 a share. You have reason to think DDRM is going to make your financial dreams come true, but you also realize it's a risky trade. You know that if the stock drops much below $48.50, it means there's trouble with the trade and you'll want out. How can you be sure to get out if the stock drops below $48.50?

After buying the stock, you place another order: a stop sell order at $48.40. This tells the broker that any DDRM execution in the market for $48.40 or less is an automatic trigger to sell your shares immediately in the form of a market order—they'll be sold at the current bid, whatever that is. This will happen automatically, which means you won't have to watch the stock like a hawk just so you can bail quickly. It also means you won't be tempted to hold on just a little longer and a little longer still, hoping(!) that the stock will go back up.

TRADER TALK In general, there are two types of stop orders: ***stop-loss*** and ***stop-limit***. (Check with your broker; some brokers use slightly different names for various order types or may not offer all order types.)

A ***stop-loss*** order is an order to sell a stock if it drops to a specified price, or to buy to cover a stock you sold short if it rises to a specified price. Once the stop is triggered, the order is executed immediately at the market price (it becomes a market order).

A ***stop-limit*** order is an order to sell a stock at a specific price and no lower than that price if it drops to that price, or to buy to cover a stock sold short at a specific price and no higher than that price if it rises to that price. Once the stop is triggered, the order is executed only if it can be executed at the limit price or better (it becomes a limit order).

WAXIE'S STREET SMARTS

Don't use stop-limit orders. There's no good reason to do it, and it needlessly increases your risk. If a stock's price is dropping fast, chances are great that a stop-limit order won't execute at all.

Let's say DDRM does drop instead of making your dreams come true. It hits $48.40, and your stop is triggered. Your stop order becomes a market order to sell. This means that it will execute immediately at the current bid price.

The same principles apply to stops on short positions. If you sell Fester Corp. short at $13, expecting it to go down, you'll place a stop buy-to-cover order at, say, $13.75. If Fester suddenly goes on a feverish rally, you're protected—and you can always reshort the stock at a higher price when you believe it's cooled off.

TRADER TALK To ***stop out*** of a position means to exit the position because your stop order has been executed.

A Few More Things to Know About Stops

Let's go back to the long position in DDRM for a minute to see what might happen. If the stock is falling slowly, the market order may execute at $48.40, slightly lower, or even slightly higher (in theory—although this doesn't happen too often). If it's falling quickly, it could execute a little below $48.40. If the stock is falling like a brick, it could execute a little below $48.40 or quite a ways below it.

This is one reason some people avoid using stops: They don't like the possibility that they could stop out far below the trigger price. Although this does have the potential to suck, what's the alternative? Would you rather keep holding the stock while it goes *even lower*? I don't think so! Besides, in most cases you'll stop out quite near your trigger price.

The one exception to the rule of having stops in place at all times is that you should never leave a stop in place overnight. The reason is the opening gaps up and down (see Chapters 3 and 4). If the stock gaps down, this volatility can needlessly cause your stop order to be filled as much as 20 percent below the price where the stock will eventually stabilize that day. This is discussed in more detail below in the section on trailing stops.

In addition to fearing a bad execution price, some people are afraid that, following some corollary to Murphy's Law, the stock will start to go back up immediately after their stop sell order's been executed. Setting stops *under* support levels, as discussed below, will help avoid this problem. A stock may still occasionally bounce right at the point where you set your stop, just as a random occurrence, but the smart trader weighs this occasional frustration against all the times she'll save *much* more money by using stops to get out of losing positions. Think of it as the cost of insurance.

How Stops Will Save Your Butt on Losing Trades

Stops limit your risk of loss on bad trades. Put another way, stops enforce the important discipline of taking small losses and getting out when stocks go against you. Some traders find that they are unwilling to take a loss on any stock. They don't want to admit that they were wrong. Who does? I sure don't. But staying in a bad trade and letting it lose you money is sheer pigheadedness. I'd rather admit I'm wrong than have my stubbornness cost me a bundle.

What often separates a good trader from a bad one is *the ability to take small losses*. Your goal must be to take small losses and make big gains. If you do this diligently, you'll become a profitable trader. But, you ask, what if you stop out of a stock you still want to trade? The answer's simple: You can always buy it back later, most likely at a better price, if the trade still has potential.

Seems like common sense, doesn't it? What's the big deal? But so many traders just don't want to bother setting stops, or are afraid they'll stop out of some great trade. Also, many traders are unsure of where—how tightly—to set their stops. It's true that setting stops is an imprecise science and involves lots of trial and error, but in this it's no different from buying insurance for your property or your health. Should you avoid insurance altogether just because you're not sure exactly how much something is worth, or because it will cost you a little money? I think not! You estimate and do the best you can, and the insurance will cost you something—of course!—but it will be well worth it. I'll tell you more about where and how to set stops below.

And again, remember what I told you in the last chapter. If you want to trade, you *must* be able to take small losses. You don't need to win on every trade. And never, never marry a stock!

RULES OF THE GAME   Be able to take small losses.
RULES OF THE GAME   You don't need to win on every trade.
RULES OF THE GAME   Don't marry stocks.

How Stops Will Save Your Butt on Winning Trades

Besides limiting risk and helping you take small losses, stops are incredibly valuable because they can protect profits on winning trades. As I said in the last chapter, you must develop the discipline of locking in profits. You can enforce this discipline using one simple technique: trailing stops.

RULES OF THE GAME   Lock in profits religiously. No *one ever went broke taking profits!*

Remember how Mr. Loser managed to make a winning trade on Orbit Galactic Corp. but then lose all his profits and more?

How can you prevent that from happening to you? (And believe me, if you don't have a plan, it will happen.) The answer is to use *trailing stops.* This means that once you have a profit, you move your stop nearer to the current price so you'll stop out with most of your profits intact if the stock turns south. What if the stop executes and you decide you want to trade the stock again? Easy: You buy it back at a better price than you sold it for, and then ride it up again. That's how a good trader makes and keeps money.

TRADER TALK   A *trailing stop* is a stop order you place below the current price of a long position, progressively moving it up as the price of the stock increases so that the stop follows the stock up. For a short position, you set a stop above the current price and then move it progressively down, following the stock as it dies.

The Mechanics of Setting Stops

Setting stops is both an art and a science, and there aren't many hard and fast rules to follow. Here are a few guidelines to keep in mind as you practice and develop the skill of setting stops.

Be aware of individual brokers' rules

Some brokers have rules about where stops can be set. For example, some have a rule that protective stops must be set at least a minimum amount below the current bid when you're long (stop sell), or above the current ask when you're short (stop buy-to-cover). For example, the rule may be that a stop sell order must be at least .25 below the current bid. This is generally not a problem with a high-priced stock, but with a very cheap stock, when every quarter-point is worth a lot relative to the share price, you might not be able to set a tight stop unless you wait for the bid to move up. In addition, if the price of a stock is dropping quickly, the bid may come too close to the stop you're trying to place before you're able to place it, causing your order to be rejected.

Another rule some brokers have is that stops can't be set more than a certain percentage lower than the current bid (or, on a short, higher than the current ask)—for example, no more than 30 percent lower (or higher). I have no idea why you'd *ever* want to lose 30 percent of the value of your trade before stopping out, and I would *never* set a stop anywhere near that low.

Keep your wits about you

You'd think it would be impossible to place a limit order when you mean to place a stop, but it's actually quite possible when you're in a hurry. Since you should be in the habit of using limit orders to enter positions, placing them should be almost second nature. That's why you need to make sure you don't enter a limit order out of habit when you mean to place a stop-loss. If you place a limit sell order at a price below the current bid (at the place where you meant to place your stop), it will execute right away and you'll be out of the trade.

NEWBIE TRAP   When you're in a hurry, it's easy to place a limit order out of habit when you mean to place a stop order. Always review orders carefully before placing them. Look at your order again and think it through one last time!

Don't set stops overnight

Remember what you read in Chapter 4 about the NASDAQ's volatility at market open? Most mornings, NASDAQ stocks either gap up or gap down from their prices at the previous day's close, and then they swing pretty wildly as overnight market orders (placed by the foolish) are filled. For example, a stock could close at 33, open the next day at 32.8, drop to 31.94, and then bounce back up to 33.15 before stabilizing and finding its direction. It could also close at 33 after a good day, open the next day at 33.75, spike up to 34.50, and then drop back to 33.60. Or it could close at 33, open at 32.8, and then spike up to 34.12 before dropping back to 33.8. You get the idea.

If you have an overnight stop in place on a long position, it's likely to be triggered by the morning's volatility, which will stop you out at the low end just before the stock bounces back up. You need to assume that there will be a gap at market open and remove your stops after the market closes, resetting them after the opening volatility the next morning so they will protect you from real downside rather than routine fake-outs. *Don't leave stops on overnight.*

You might also consider doing what lots of traders do, especially when the market has no consistent direction: simply avoid holding many positions overnight. Once you get better at anticipating what will probably happen the next day (realizing that there can always be overnight surprises)—and at recognizing when there's no way to anticipate what will happen—you'll feel more comfortable making these judgment calls. As always, if you don't have a pretty good idea what will happen, it's best to avoid the situation completely: *When in doubt, stay out!*

N E W B I E   T R A P Don't place tight good-until-canceled or overnight stop orders that will be triggered by the volatility of a gap up or gap down at market open. Wait until the market has stabilized (after 10 A.M.) before tightening your stops for the day.

WAXIE'S STREET SMARTS

If you'll be unable to trade for several days (for example, while you're on vacation), consider whether it makes more sense to set stops or to exit your positions altogether. Unless you're in a great long-term trend trade and the market has a definite direction, it may be better to exit all positions and start fresh when you return to trading.

Decide how tightly to set stops

The most important question about setting stops is how tightly you should set them—how close to the price where you entered the position or, for trailing stops, how close to the current price. This is a general decision you'll make before you figure out exactly what price will be your stop trigger. How tightly to set stops depends on several factors:

- **How much you're willing to lose on a single trade**. My rule is that *you should never lose more than 2 percent of your trading capital on any one trade.*

- **How risky you believe the trade is.** If you think the trade is a sure winner and market conditions are favorable, you may give the stock more room to move down before triggering a stop. If you think it's got only a fair chance of working out, or if the stock has serious tankage potential, set a tight stop (or don't make the trade at all).

- **How volatile the stock is.** If the stock routinely moves up and down in a range of 15 percent or more over the course of the day, even when it's not really going anywhere, you can't set tight stops. If you do, you'll be knocked out of the position by the stock's normal volatility. If the stock is choppy but too risky to trade without tight stops, maybe you'd better look for a better stock to trade.

- **How cheap the stock is.** When a stock is dirt cheap, even the smallest decimal price movement will be fairly large in percentage terms. This means tight stops may be knocked out more easily. It also means that if your broker has a rule that you can't set a stop closer than .25 below the current bid, you may not be able to set a tight stop until the price moves up.

- **How much money you have in the play.** You should consider this in conjunction with the rule that you should never lose more than 2 percent of your capital on any one trade. If you have a large amount of money in a play, 2 percent may be much more than you're willing to lose. If so, you should set stops accordingly. If your account is small and you're not well diversified, a 2 percent stop may be so tight that you may stop out immediately. If this is the case, you should review Chapter 2 and think seriously about whether you have enough money to trade.

- **Market conditions.** If the bulls are running like exuberant wild things, tight stops may not be necessary. If you're trying to go long in a bearish market, tight stops are absolutely necessary. If the market is choppy—if it has no clear direction or if it's full of nervousness and fear—use tight stops (and ask yourself whether you should be trading at all that day).

- **The time frame for the trade.** On a quick day trade, tight stops are a good idea. On a stock you expect to hold for a week or two for a trend play, they may or may not be, depending on other factors you're aware of.

- **What you have reason to think will happen to the stock.** If you have reason to be confident that the stock will move upward even if it swings around a bit first, it doesn't make sense to set a tight stop because you'll just stop out as it swings. If you think it might possibly move up but will definitely tank if it slips below a certain price, then tight stops are a must.

WAXIE'S STREET SMARTS

Never lose more than 2 percent of your trading capital on any single trade.

Which of these considerations is most important? Since no two trades are the same, different factors will dominate on different trades. Think about all of them on every trade. If you don't, you'll miss something important. Your job is to exercise good trading judgment and figure out what makes sense for each trade. This is where the "art" of setting stops comes in: You have to experiment a bit and learn what works for you. You'll occasionally stop out of a trade too soon and feel frustrated, but remember: *This is just the price of insurance and, at least at first, of education.* You'll get better and better at setting stops as time goes on.

Your ultimate goal is to develop flexibility in your thinking so that each new situation makes sense to you on its own terms. This is how you'll become a nimble trader who can trade *with* the market.

Set stop sell orders below support

The one fairly specific rule in setting stop sells—the "science" part—is that you should not set them either right on the stock's support level or just above support. Instead, unless the support level is so low that stopping out there would lose you too high a percentage of your capital, set stops *below* support.

TRADER TALK   A *support level* is a price at which the stock has previously bounced (reversed its downward course). Think of it as a potential floor. See the chart below for an illustration.

Micron Technology, Daily – QCharts ©2001 Quote.com

Support.

Copyright © 2001 Quote.com, Inc., a Lycos Network site. QCharts is a registered trademark of Lycos Network. All charts or trading products or services mentioned herein are those of Lycos or their respective owners. All rights reserved.

WAXIE'S STREET SMARTS
Don't set stops at or slightly above a support level. Set them *below* support.

The reason it's so important to set stops *below* support is that stocks moving downward tend to bounce upward (reverse course) at or near their support levels. They may later begin to move downward again, break through support, and continue to move even lower. *A clear break below support is dictated by where a stock closes, not by intraday swings*. Alternatively, after bouncing off support, a stock may continue to move upward, never returning to the support level at all. For purposes of setting stops, it doesn't make sense to set a stop right at support because the stock is almost certain to bounce up from that point, possibly reversing course. If you set your stop below support, it probably won't be triggered unless the stock has broken support and will continue downward.

WAXIE'S STREET SMARTS
A clear break below support is dictated by where a stock closes, not by intraday swings.

The same principle applies for a stop buy-to-cover on a short position: Set your stop *above,* not at or below, resistance.

T R A D E R   T A L K   A *resistance level* is a price at which the stock has previously reversed its upward course. Think of it as a potential ceiling. See the chart on page 180 for an illustration.

WAXIE'S STREET SMARTS
A clear break above resistance is dictated by where a stock closes, not by intraday swings.

Motorola Inc, Daily — QCharts ©2001 Quote.com

Resistance.

As a general rule, an old resistance level that's been broken through on an upward trend will serve as a new support level. Likewise, an old support level that's been broken through on a downward trend will serve as a new resistance level.

WAXIE'S STREET SMARTS

As a general rule, old resistance becomes a new support when resistance is broken and old support becomes new resistance when support is lost.

Intel Corporation (NM), Weekly – QCharts ©2001 Quote.com

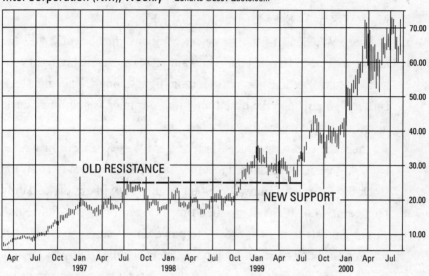

Old resistance becomes new support.
Copyright © 2001 Quote.com, Inc., a Lycos Network site. QCharts is a registered trademark of Lycos Network. All charts or trading products or services mentioned herein are those of Lycos or their respective owners. All rights reserved.

Example: Protective Stop and Trailing Stops

Here's an example to illustrate the reasoning behind decisions about where to set protective and trailing stop sells.

Protective stop

First, to illustrate the importance of setting stop sells below support: Let's say you take a long position in Web Acknowledgement Ltd. (WACK) in anticipation of its earnings announcement. It had traded at around 13 for many weeks, but last week it ran up to 16, probably as the first sign of its earnings run. It then slowly dropped to 14.4 over the course of two days and stabilized there for a day and a half. Today it's started to slowly move up again, and you think it'll keep going. You decide now's the time to buy. You put in a limit buy order for WACK at 14.8, and it executes at 14.76.

Since WACK isn't the strongest company in the world and the market has been iffy of late, you want to set a reasonably tight protective stop. You don't want to set it too tight, though, since the stock isn't too volatile and the time frame for your trade is about five days. You look to see where the stock has support.

There are two support levels: 13, where WACK traded for weeks, and 14.4, where it stabilized recently. Its resistance level is 16. If the stock moves down from where you bought it, it will almost certainly bounce at 14.4. If the stock then drops *below* 14.4, you figure that would indicate that it isn't ready to move up yet, and you'd be better off stopping out there and rebuying later. For this reason, you also figure there's no reason to let the stock move all the way down to 13. Since its support at 13 is very solid, any drop through the floor at 13 would mean a real weakness had developed in the stock.

You decide to set a protective stop at 13.75. You don't want to set it right at 14.4, since it's almost sure to bounce near 14.4 and then either start back up or continue down. You don't want to set it above 14.4 for the same reason. You choose 13.75 because no support level is absolute, and WACK could bounce off 14.3, 14.5, or any number close to them as easily as it could bounce off 14.4. If the stock gets as low as 13.75, though, that would suggest that the stock will actually break through support. (Remember, the rule is that a clear break of support is dictated by where a stock closes, not by intraday swings.)

Trailing stops

You made a good call! WACK motors up to 15.1, stays there a while, suddenly dips sharply to 14.43, and then picks up volume and really goes to town. It breaks through its new resistance at 15 and starts the climb to 16. The market is rallying.

Now's the time to start to think about using trailing stops to protect your profit. You're starting to accumulate a nice one: At 15.50,
you've made 5 percent, and if the stock hits 16.24, your profit will be
10 percent. You decide that the stock should stay above its old resistance of around 15 unless trouble is brewing. (Now that the stock has
broken through its old resistance at 15, that price will serve as a new
support level. Remember, old resistance becomes new support.) You
move your stop up to 14.85.

The stock could pull back a bit at 16, since that level served as the
ceiling before. When the stock nears 16, you'll have a choice: either
take profits by selling out directly or setting a very tight trailing stop,
or increase the looser stop trigger to 15.3 in anticipation of a further
move upward.

You decide that, since at 16 WACK will already have moved up
almost 25 percent from its longtime price of 13, it may not blow
through 16 so easily. You decide to set a tight stop once it hits 16
instead of selling out, just to give it a chance. So once WACK hits
15.7, you move your stop up to 15.2; when it hits 16, you move the
stop up to 15.75. Surprise! The market's rally intensifies after great
earnings reports from three leading companies, and WACK runs up
to 16.73 before it begins to sputter. You quickly sell out at 16.68 for
a nice 13 percent profit.

If WACK had pulled back after hitting 16, you would have
stopped out at 15.75 with a profit of nearly 7 percent. You could then
have rebought the stock if it dropped even lower *and* you were still
convinced that it would eventually move up again. Both scenarios
rock!

Why Are Support and Resistance Levels Significant?

What's so special about the prices that act as support and resistance points? Is there something all the insiders know about the company's valuation at those levels? Do they give some clue as to the real value of the company?

It's really nothing of the sort. There's absolutely nothing special about a number like 13 or 14.4 for WACK, or any support or resistance level for any stock. They're more like self-fulfilling prophecies. Basically, everyone in the market, from mutual fund managers to market makers to you, is looking at the same charts. Everyone expects stocks to bounce off support because a support level is a price that is identifiable. The reason it has significance is because it is identifiable, and everyone reading the charts will identify it. Because everyone expects the stock to bounce off support, it usually will.

It really is as simple as that.

The Comeback Kid: How to Recover from a Bad Loss

There's no such thing as a perfect trader. If your goal is to be perfect, then trading is more about your ego than it is about making money. Every trader on the planet makes a mistake from time to time. I've made some whoppers, even after I got pretty good at trading. The good news is that the better you get and the more experienced you become, the fewer mistakes you'll make. If you're using stops on all your trades, even a few bad mistakes shouldn't wipe you out. Instead of perfection, your goals should be to improve continually and use proper techniques and money management consistently.

While it's in your power to prevent avoidable mistakes, you must also realize that some market events can't be fully anticipated or planned for. Things can change very quickly—one example that comes to mind is Alan Greenspan's surprise interest-rate cut in early January 2001, which *absolutely no one* saw coming. If you stay alert and nimble and have stops in place, these quick changes shouldn't hurt you badly. But it's always possible to be completely blindsided, to have a disastrous computer crash or other equipment outage at just the wrong time, or simply to be unable to exit a large position quickly enough. On occasion, it's also possible to be just plain wrong about something you felt very confident about. Things can happen that aren't your fault, and they can make you sustain a large loss.

If you ever suffer a large loss, take the following steps:

- *First, take some time off from trading.* Just do something else for a while—ideally, a week or two. It's healthy to have some time away from it all before you get back on the horse.

- *Analyze and learn from the experience.* Setbacks are great learning opportunities. Take advantage of the lessons offered by the experience, and figure out how to keep the same thing from happening again.

- *Make necessary adjustments to your trading strategy.* Figure out whether a weakness in money management or strategy contributed to the problem. Figure out how to correct the problem, and fix it.

- *Trade on paper or in a simulated account for a while before resuming actual trading.* You need to feel comfortable and in control before you start trading your account again. You've been shaken emotionally, and you need to get your confidence back. Besides that, your time off from trading will have left you a little out of touch with the market when you return, and it's better to get up to speed without risking capital. Get emotionally and intellectually comfortable by making simulated trades for a while.

- *Treat the experience as a thing of the past that won't affect future trades.* Don't keep spooking yourself by reminding yourself of the disaster. The only way to trade successfully is to trade with confidence. If you're feeling guilty or are scared of a repeat disaster, you won't be able to trade with a winning attitude.

- *Treat your return to actual trading as a new start, free of pressure to regain lost capital.* Whatever you do, don't keep punishing and distracting yourself by trying to "make up for the loss." As far as the size of your account is concerned, forget that the loss ever happened. Each day is a brand-new day. Don't muddy your thinking by putting pressure on yourself to "undo" it.

- *Maintain a winning attitude and make only trades in which you have confidence.* This is the attitude and approach you should always have when trading. You need to regain it and sustain it in order to continue trading.

The Most Important Lesson in This Entire Book

If you take only one lesson from this whole book, let it be this one: Always, always, *always* use stop-loss orders on your trades. Emblazon these three words on your brain and tape them to your computer: *Always use stops!*

RULES OF THE GAME   *Always* use stops!

Exercises

Spend some time thinking about the following concepts. Use actual price examples as you think about them.

I. Differences Between Stop and Limit Orders

Stop orders and limit orders aren't exact opposites of each other. Think about the differences between stop and limit orders. Commit the following points to memory:

- The basic idea behind limit orders is that you don't want to buy or sell unless you can get your price or better.

- The basic idea behind stop-loss orders is that once the pain of loss has reached your trigger point, you want out right away at whatever price you're offered.

II. Stop and Limit Order Scenarios

Work through some price examples to make sure you understand the following scenarios. Draw pictures to help you visualize the price relationships.

For long positions:

- If you place a limit buy order below the current ask price, it won't be executed until the ask reaches your limit price or better.

- If you place a limit buy order above the current ask price, it will be executed immediately at the current ask because the current ask is better than your limit price.

- If you place a stop sell order below the price of the stock's last trade, it won't be executed until someone else's order is executed at or below your stop price.

- If you place a stop sell order above the price of the stock's last trade, it will be executed right away (unless your broker rejects it) because the current price is lower than your stop price.

For short positions:

- If you place a limit sell short order above the current bid price, it won't execute until the bid reaches your limit price or better. (You want to sell short at the highest possible price. See Chapter 10 for a full explanation of selling short.)

- If you place a limit sell short order below the current bid price, it will execute immediately at the current bid because the current bid is better than your limit price.

- If you place a stop buy-to-cover order above the price of the stock's last trade, it won't execute until the current price rises to your stop price. (You want to buy to cover at the lowest possible price. The purpose of your stop is to prevent the purchase from becoming so expensive that you lose a lot of money.)

- If you place a stop buy-to-cover order below the price of the stock's last trade, it will be executed right away (unless your broker rejects it) because the current price is higher than your stop price.

Every time you get ready to place a stop or limit order, think through exactly what will happen if the price goes up from where it is now, and what will happen if the price goes down from where it is now.

Chapter 10

Short and Sweet

Flexibility in Volatile Markets

....
This chapter covers:

- Why you must learn to sell stocks short
- What it means to short a stock
- Differences between shorting and regular (long) buying and selling
- Importance of setting stops
- Mechanics of shorting
- How to pick good shorts and avoid bad ones
- Psychological barriers to shorting
- Exercise in picking short plays

TRADER TALK *Taking a stock long* means buying a stock with the expectation that its price will go up.

Selling a stock short means selling a borrowed stock with the expectation that its price will go down.

Switching Sides: Why You Must Learn to Sell Stocks Short

Mama said there would be days like this. Boy, was she right.

All of a sudden the market abandons the good times like last week's fishhead stew and starts screaming downward, straight toward the bowels of hell. It just goes down, down, down like there's never been another way to go. You realize that we're having a major, big-time, grab-the-lifeboats correction.

Every stock on the board is down 15 percent, 20 percent, 30 percent—even more. Even the ones *everybody* respects. The NASDAQ is down many percentage points for the day—maybe 5 percent, maybe twice that much.

When a bloodbath happens, it happens fast and ugly.

Why is this happening? you ask. Maybe the market has soared for weeks, to the point where no one believes the stocks' valuations make any sense. When the market is thoroughly bloated and stock prices are puffed up like thousands of piping hot soufflés, just about any news that's less than stellar will send institutions and investors fleeing for the exits. Or maybe an international financial crisis suddenly threatens to derail the economy, creating the specter of global recession and all kinds of worldwide gloom and doom. Or maybe Alan Greenspan just scratched his nose three times today instead of two.

Whatever the reason, chances are that this eye-popping crash was not the first sign of trouble. Like the sky before a bad thunderstorm, the market may have been clouding up for weeks. There may be more talk of overvaluation. Analysts may all be saying that a correction is needed to get prices back to reasonable levels. The market may have adopted a recent pattern of going down more than up. Those who kept an eye on the darkening heavens may have quietly started bringing their toys in from the yard in case of rain—selling most of their stocks and assuming a largely cash position to protect their capital.

You may be one of the sellers. Maybe you started to unload your stocks when you saw that the market had run up so fast and become so inflated that you knew it couldn't last much longer. More likely, though, you've taken a hit. No one can guess exactly when the market will correct, and it doesn't really make sense to try, though there are trends that can give you great clues. But even if you've taken a hit, it won't be a huge loss, since you're a responsible trader who *always sets stops* to protect yourself against just such a conflagration. You've now stopped out of all your positions. At least, let's *hope* you did!

The most important thing, always, is to survive to trade another day. Your capital is your lifeblood. If it's lost, the patient is dead.

At this point, the good news is that you're not going down in flames with the rest of the market. The bad news, though, is that the market just keeps falling like the rain in Spain, and you're starting to freak because you see it's impossible to make any ka-chingos by buying stocks. The analysts on TV keep telling everyone to "buy the dip," but they have no clue what kind of dip this is—is it a true market bottom, or just the middle of a long downhill slide? Every time you buy, your stocks tank along with the rest of the market and you stop out, again and again. Those small losses are adding up, and it's really frustrating. This bad market weather can go on for days at a time, with short one-day relief rallies that are just convincing enough to fool you into letting down your guard and buying just as the rally evaporates. That will be the dominant pattern when the market is trending downward. A real correction can last for weeks, even months. A bear market can last much longer—even years (the average bear market lasts about eighteen months).

So the question is, *what do you do?* How can you make good money in a sinking market?

There's only one thing to do when the market tanks, and that's to sell stocks short.

When the market's in the middle of a spirit-crushing trip to lower ground, you *cannot* buck the trend and try to buy stocks. In a correction, even the strongest, highest-quality stocks will eventually begin to lose value. The party train has gone into reverse, and it's picking up speed. You can't stop it, and if you try, you'll be crushed beneath its wheels. Instead, you have to *climb aboard and ride*!

And how do you ride the train on its journey back down the hill?

To ride a stock downward and profit from the trip, you have to *sell it short.*

RULES OF THE GAME   Be flexible. *Don't fight the market!*

What It Means to Short a Stock

So, exactly what *is* short selling?

Selling a stock short means that you sell it without first owning it. You do this when you expect the stock's price to go down. Here's how it works: By selling short, you're borrowing the stock from your broker and selling it when you think the price is as high as it's going to be for a while. When the price goes down, you close the position by buying shares—to replace the ones you borrowed and sold—at a lower price than you sold them for. Borrow shares and sell them high; buy them back lower and return them. *Ka-chingo!*

Here's another way to look at it. Instead of buying low and then selling high, you just do the same thing in reverse order: Sell high, and then buy low. Same price difference, just in reverse order because the price is moving down instead of up.

Here's an example: Let's say you think the stock of Dot-com Goldrush Corp. (symbol WEAK) is going to head down. The price is $35. You sell 100 shares short at $35 and wait. The next day you're ecstatic when WEAK takes a dive on an analyst's downgrade and slides to $27. *Die, WEAK!* At this point you're not sure it will go down anymore, so you buy the 100 shares back at $27 to close the trade. Your bargain-basement purchase of WEAK has given you the difference between a $27 purchase and a $35 sale—eight dollars per share, for a total return of $800.

Kill the stocks! Kill the stocks! Die, die, die!

Differences Between Selling Short and Buying Long

There aren't too many differences between shorting and buying long, but there are a few important ones.

1. Margin status.

A short sale is a margin transaction. This is because you have to borrow shares from your broker to sell short, and borrowing means you have to be approved for margin. If you don't have a margin account, you can't sell short.

2. Price limits.

Your broker may allow you to short only stocks above a certain price—for example, only stocks costing five dollars or more per share. And you can short only the stocks that your broker considers "marginable." You also can't short initial public offerings (IPOs) until thirty days after they've started trading.

3. Share availability.

There will be times when your broker has no shares of a particular stock available for you to borrow. When this happens, you're just plain out of luck.

4. The "uptick rule."

The uptick rule is a Securities Exchange Commission rule that allows short selling only where the most recent bid on the stock is an "uptick," meaning that it is higher than the bid that came just before it.

For example, let's say the bid on FiscalChaos.com (DEBT) is at 12.63. If the bid appears on the screen in green or is shown next to an uptick symbol (a plus sign or up arrow), it represents an increase in share value over the previous bid—an uptick. For example, if the previous bid was 12.50, then the bid of 12.63 would be an uptick. With such an uptick, you can short DEBT at 12.63.

If the bid of 12.63 appears in red or is shown next to a downtick symbol (a minus sign or down arrow), though, you cannot short it at 12.63. (A downtick, as you've probably figured out, is a bid that's lower than the previous bid. Here, the bid may have gone from 12.75 to 12.63.) In this situation you can try to short DEBT at 12.64, because if the bid goes from 12.63 to 12.64 it will create an uptick.

The bottom line is that you have to wait for an uptick in order to sell short. As soon as the bid rises by any amount, it's an uptick and the stock is shortable for as long as that bid or any bid following it remains an uptick. Another way to state the rule is that you can't short on a downtick.

5. Terminology.

When you sell short, you don't "sell" a stock and then "buy" it back. Instead, you first *sell the stock short* and then *buy to cover*. These are the types of orders you must place to open and close a short position.

6. Reward.

When you buy a stock long and it goes up in price, it can—at least in theory—keep going up forever. No stock on planet Earth will really go up *forever,* but a good stock can go up 200 percent, 500 percent, or even more—sometimes in a short time, sometimes over a period of years.

When you short a stock, though, the situation is a bit different. If you think about it, the best possible outcome when you hold a short position is for the stock to go to zero. Most stocks won't go to zero, but they can lose half their value or even three-fourths of it. If a stock loses half its value, your return is 50 percent. If it loses three-fourths of its value, your return is 75 percent. If it actually goes to zero (because the company goes out of business entirely, let's say), your return is 100 percent. But your return on a short can never be more than 100 percent.

(Another limitation to the return on a short is that, since every short sale is a margin transaction, you can't increase the size of your positions by borrowing additional shares on margin because you've already borrowed shares on margin. When you go long, you can borrow against the shares and, at least theoretically, double your return or better. When you sell short, you hold nothing to borrow against because the shares are already borrowed. This means you can never sell short an amount of stock whose value exceeds the value of your account.)

On the other hand, stocks tend to fall faster than they rise, so you may get your return on a short sooner.

So there's a limit to the return you can make on a short, while there's theoretically no limit on the return you can make going long. Realistically, though, a 10 percent to 30 percent return is a pretty good ka-chingo for any trade, long or short. It's entirely possible to make that kind of profit with a good short, and it's the same return you'll make on the majority of long plays, anyway. And the beauty of being a trader is that you'll limit your loss either way by using stops.

7. Risk.

The most important difference between buying long and selling short is the magnitude of risk involved. This is the flip side of the difference in reward discussed above. When you buy a stock long, the most you can possibly lose is 100 percent of your money. With a short, though, the theoretical possibility of loss is infinite. In other words, in theory (but not in practice), there is no limit to what a bad short can cost you.

For example, let's say you're convinced that the price of Lameways, Inc. is going to go down. You have your reasons, and they're sound, and the time is right. So you short 500 shares of LAME at $10 per share—a $5000 investment—and sit back to wait for the big crash. The price goes down some, and you're comfortably cheering it on to its shameful demise. *Die, you dog!*

Well—wouldn't you know—the very next afternoon LAME announces that it's just signed a contract to be the primary supplier of turbo-cyberwidgets to the world's biggest purchaser of the freaking things—a contract worth $100 million a year for the next three years. For LAME, this is the contract of a lifetime. The stock goes to $15 that day, and the next day hits $20.

If, for some inexplicable reason, you did not set stops, what does this mean for you? You guessed it—Disasterville. If you bought the stock at $10 and it's now $20, your loss is equal to exactly the amount of your investment. This is because, if you shorted 500 LAME at $10, you borrowed $5000 worth of stock. (This is what you "paid" for your investment, in effect, because it's the amount you put into the trade.) If you have to buy it back at $20, the cost will be $10,000: a $5000 loss. You have to replace the borrowed stock at whatever price it takes to get hold of the shares. If you replace the shares at $20, you have lost your entire investment.

Suppose, though, that you decide to wait to cover, *hoping* (yikes!) that the price will go down. Unfortunately, the stock continues to climb. Let's say it hits $30. Now you've lost *twice* as much as you invested in the first place. If the stock continues up to $40, you lose three times your investment. And so it goes, in theory, up to infinity.

Your Position in This Game Is Always Short Stop

Now, before you swear that you'll never be moronic enough to sell a stock short and take on infinite risk, there's one important thing to consider: *If you set stops on a short, the risk is no different than it is for a long position.* Any time you short, you *must* follow the same rule you follow on every play: *You must set stops!* If your stops are in place, you'll automatically limit your loss and avoid Disasterville.

Some people like to point out that no stock *really* goes to infinity, and that even if it did, it would probably take more than a day or two to get there. That's true. At the same time, a bad short doesn't need to go to anywhere near infinity to leave your account as empty as a nuclear winter, and some stocks do climb like overachieving mountain goats. If you let a bad short get completely out of control, this is what will happen: Your broker will give you a margin call before you can owe *too* much more than your account's value, you'll cover the short at a huge and painful loss, and, as for your account, it'll be all over but the shouting. The point is that there's *never* a good reason to take chances. I'll repeat it until you hear it in your own head: *You must always set stops.*

·····························

WAXIE'S STREET SMARTS

Assuming that you're setting stops religiously, as you must, the only way you can really get into trouble with a short is if the stock price gaps up tremendously overnight in response to some news and you don't have access to premarket trading. A stock's price can change rapidly in the half hour before the market opens, and there's not much you can do if you can't trade during that half hour. For this reason, you should never hold a short that has spent its downward momentum and stabilized at some level. You have little to gain and are risking a sudden change in the company's situation that could make you wish you'd closed the position with a profit.

It's Time to Try It: The Mechanics of Shorting

If you've never shorted before, please go slowly. You should try a few short sales in a simulated online portfolio or on paper before you jump in with real money. The more comfortable you are with the entire process, the clearer your thinking will be.

The mechanics of a short sale are the same as a normal sale, except that you must sell on an uptick and use the appropriate type of order.

Step 1: Sell short using a limit order.

Always, *always* use a limit order when selling short. A limit "sell short" order will guarantee that you will not sell short for less than the price you indicate. By contrast, using market orders to sell short is *extremely* hazardous because of the uptick rule. If you use a market sell short order and the stock's price starts to fall quickly, there can be a long series of consecutive downticks that will prevent your order from being filled. If the price has fallen significantly before an uptick occurs, you will end up shorting the stock at a much lower price than you wanted to, and probably near its low point—just as it's getting ready to bounce back up.

For example, let's say you try to short Pigdog, Inc. (DAWG) with a market order at 45.63. The stock is on a downtick, and then it begins to fall quickly. The bid keeps going lower and lower (downtick after downtick, with no uptick) until the stock finally bounces (an uptick) at 36.5. Your order executes at 36.5. DAWG is now 20 percent lower than the price where you wanted to short it. Not only is most or all of your potential gain gone, but you are in danger of shorting at exactly the point where the slide stops and the stock begins to bounce back up.

Using a limit order to short DAWG works this way. Let's say you set your limit order at 45.63. If there is an uptick on the bid at 45.63, your order will execute at 45.63 because your limit order allows you to sell at 45.63 or higher. If the bid of 45.63 is a downtick, then the order will fill only if the bid moves up to 45.64, or if the bid drops below 45.63 and later moves back up to 45.63 on an uptick.

Step 2: Set a stop immediately.

Once your short sale order has filled, you should immediately place a stop buy-to-cover order. This is your protection from a sudden rise in price that could cause a huge loss.

Step 3: Close the short position by buying to cover.

When it's time to close the short position, you simply place a buy-to-cover order—you should normally use limit orders here, as well—for the same number of shares you sold short. (An exception is if the company completed a stock split while you held the short position; in that case, you must buy the number of shares you held short after the split. For example, if you shorted 200 DAWG on March 1, the stock split two for one on May 1, and you wanted to cover on June 1, you'd need to cover by buying 400 DAWG. This situation is discussed further at the end of this chapter.)

Some brokerages won't let you use regular "buy" order to cover a short. If this is your broker's rule and you do use a buy order, you'll end up with both a short position *and* a long position. Their gains and losses will cancel each other out, but you'll tie up lots of money for no reason.

A buy-to-cover order is not subject to any sort of uptick rule or other complication. In terms of mechanics, it's just like buying any stock. Only the type of order is different.

You see, it's not so hard! Try a few short sales in a simulated trading account or on paper, and then try a small one in your real account. When I tried my first short, I made it a small one. I looked at it as a new experience—like trying cotton candy for the first time, or Indian food, or skinny-dipping! *Yeah, baby!* As always, sell a stock short *only* if you believe it's a winning trade. *Always have a plan, and always set a stop.*

Finding a Winning Short Play

As with taking a stock long, the two aspects of shorting that will contribute most to your success are *having a good reason for the play* and *entering at the right price.*

Good reasons for a short

A stock might be a good shorting candidate for any of a number of reasons. The more of these reasons you see in a play, the better your chances of success. In other words, three sound reasons are better than one, and four are better still.

In general, one of the best times to short is when the market is really tanking. On a day when the NASDAQ is in the negative by over 150 points, chances are good that any stock still showing a gain for the day will eventually succumb to selling pressure—unless it has risen for an unusually compelling, company-specific reason.

On the other hand, a raging-bull rally is generally *not* a good climate for shorting, no matter how weak the stock, unless—again—there's a company-specific reason. *Remember, you can't fight the market.* And "choppy" days, when the market can't make up its mind on direction but instead swings back and forth between positive and negative territory, aren't great days to trade at all—long or short—because it's so easy to be whipsawed by quick reversals and lose money no matter what you try to do.

It's often a good idea to short on days when the market is in a stinky, bearish mood, or even a full-blown correction. Even on brutally negative days, though, keep in mind that the market can reverse direction very, very quickly, and often when you least expect it. *Always* use stops on your shorts to guard against disastrous bullish surprises. And you can short selectively even on rally days, since stocks will be running up on news—allowing you to "sell the news."

Aside from general market conditions, the things to look for in a potential short play are generally company-specific, or at least sector-specific.

When bears rule the market, the best stocks to short are those that have run up a lot—say, 40 percent or more in a day—on fairly trivial news. These stocks tend to drop back very quickly when day traders sell, seeing no more upside potential, and other short sellers move in. Here's an example: Me-Too Fiber Optic, Inc., a company with serious financial troubles, announces that it has received a small order from a large customer. This is not exactly earth-shattering news. Amazingly, though, the stock price is up 50 percent for the day. Especially on a negative market day, this is a very good short. As always, use a stop buy-to-cover order—if the price goes up more and you stop out, you can always reshort at a higher price.

In any market, bullish or bearish, a great time to short a stock is right when it reports earnings, unless the earnings are truly eye-popping or the stock is extremely popular. The dominant trend is for stocks to rise into earnings and fall after earnings are announced. (This is a classic example of "buy the rumor, sell the news.") The same is often true for stock splits: the price usually rises as the split date approaches, but within a day or two after the stock starts trading at its split-adjusted price, the price starts to fall. And in a bull market, a really great kind of stock to short is a parent company that has just spun off part of itself as an IPO. The parent's stock rises into the IPO, then tanks—often within minutes of the time the new issue starts to trade.

WAXIE'S STREET SMARTS

Good reasons to short:

- Rapidly falling market
- Clear break below support
- Stock has run up too far, too fast
- Rumor's been bought; it's time to sell news
- After rise into earnings
- After rise into split

- After rise into IPO spinoff

- After IPO lockup expiration

     The chart below shows the behavior of a stock that has broken below support.

Bad reasons for a short

In a bull market, there are quite a few bad reasons to short a stock. Here are some examples:

1. The company has a bad business plan and must eventually fail.

2. The stock has been "acting weak."

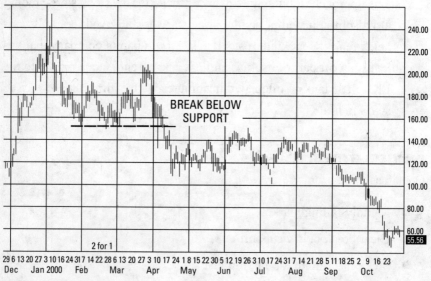

Yahoo! Inc. (NM), Daily – QCharts ©2001 Quote.com

Break below support.
Copyright © 2001 Quote.com, Inc., a Lycos Network site. QCharts is a registered trademark of Lycos Network. All charts or trading products or services mentioned herein are those of Lycos or their respective owners. All rights reserved.

3. The stock is overvalued.

4. The stock price has gone up so much that it has to go down.

What's wrong with shorting an overvalued stock? Isn't it common sense to short an issue that's overvalued, since the market must eventually bring the price down to where it belongs?

Some of the best advice I can give you is this: In the stock market, *beware of common sense*! When the bulls are running, common sense can be your worst enemy. Rational valuations and logic are *not* keys to success in an exuberant market. If anything, they'll lead you to disaster. A popular stock whose price is higher than you think it should be can keep rising in price for a year, and can easily quadruple in value before it comes back down. *You can't fight the market, and you shouldn't try.* The market is *not* efficient, and it doesn't necessarily reflect the true value of anything at any particular moment. Instead of thinking about what stocks' valuations *should* be, you have to be willing to accept what the market offers and play by its rules—by using market trends.

Psychological Barriers to Shorting

Misplaced loyalty

In some cases, the skills that serve you well in trading will also serve you well in life. For example, discipline, both in trading and in life, is incredibly important if you want to succeed. So is having a plan. If you don't have a plan in life, as in trading, you're going to end up in pretty sorry shape.

But there are some things that serve you well in life that will *not* help you thrive in the market. In fact, they will hurt you—a lot. One of these things is loyalty.

In life, loyalty is a great virtue. It's a wonderful trait to have regarding friends and family, great political causes, and baseball teams. Where I come from, you stick by your friends, and you expect them to stick by you. Loyalty to a great cause can change the world—even in our cynical times, it's hard to deny that the Underground Railroad, the World War II resistance movement, and the American civil rights movement were worthy causes that deserved loyalty. And what can I say about my beloved New York Mets? They may always be the underdogs, but I don't care. You couldn't make me a Yankees fan if the Mets never won another game.

But one thing that doesn't deserve *anyone's* loyalty is a stock. I've known lots of traders who start to develop a misplaced sense of loyalty to their "favorite" stocks, and, though it might take a while, those stocks let them down every time. Where I come from, if your friends start letting you down, you start to think twice about whether they deserve your friendship. I want to be perfectly clear: *No one should feel an ounce of loyalty to any stock, ever. All stocks suck!* Think about it! Stocks are not human. They are not your friends. Stocks *do not deserve* our affection, loyalty, or even trust. The price of a stock often has nothing at all to do with how good the company is, nothing to do with the people that work there. Any sense of loyalty toward stocks is totally misplaced.

The stock market is run by people who play it as a moneymaking game. They don't care about the companies or the investors, and they sure don't care about you. What they really want is to take your money. The goal of all stock market players is to make money, and making money always means taking money away from someone else.

As for companies, well, you'd have to be pretty naive to think that they care about you either. Do you think that the CEO of any company cares whether you make money on its stock? Should you trust a company to do things that will make your portfolio more valuable? Of course not. I'd never trust corporate America to look out for my interests, and neither should you.

Stocks can hurt you—badly—and they will never, ever feel your pain. You, and maybe your family, are the only one who will feel it. Less-than-stellar earnings can send a stock tumbling by up to 50 percent in a day. Does the company care if its earnings report loses you money? It does not. And when the market corrects, as it does several times a year, no stock is immune. They will *all* lose value. You can count on it.

That's why you have to play stocks *both ways*. When they're going up, you buy them long. When they're going down, you sell them short. They exist as tools for you to make money for the things that really do matter to you—your family, and other legitimate objects of your loyalty. Stocks are the means to an end (*use 'em and abuse 'em!*), and nothing more. It's war, and in war there's only one winner—and it's got to be us!

Belief that shorting is evil

Some people think that shorting is something only evil people do because it destroys the value of people's investments and is nothing more than taking their money.

This belief is as misplaced as loyalty to stocks. If there were no forces opposing the irrational exuberance of an out-of-control bull market, stock-price bubbles would be even more extreme than they already are (hard to imagine, isn't it?). When those bubbles eventually collapsed, the pain would be far, far worse than the corrections we experience.

Forces opposing irrational exuberance are healthy for the market because they help it stay in balance. It's like letting an opposing opinion have a voice—if there were no short selling, only bulls would be able to have their say, and bears would have no opportunity to speak. The only way to express the opinion that a stock's price was too high would be to sell it, and that option would be available only to people who already owned it.

Fear of shorting

Besides fear of infinite loss, the main source of fear in shorting is the fear of the unfamiliar. Shorting is *slightly* different from buying long, but you'll be surprised how little difference there really is. As I said above, the best way to get comfortable shorting is to start off virtual—in a simulated account, or on paper—and then small, in your real account. Always short for a reason, and always plan the entire trade. Use limit orders, and *always* set stops.

That said, I've found that there are a few people who, for whatever reason, just never get comfortable with selling short. If you find that shorting really, really doesn't work for you, then don't do it anymore. But unless you become utterly convinced that you are constitutionally unable to short, please try to develop this valuable technique. It's the most important skill to have in a bear market, and it will give you the flexibility to make consistent ka-chingos in any market. Frankly, I don't think anyone can succeed as a trader without shorting.

A Few More Notes on Shorting

Splits

If the stock you sell short has a share split while you're holding the position, the number of shorted shares in your portfolio will change. When you buy to cover, you'll just buy the new number of shares. For instance, if you short 10 shares of Tulip Tech's stock at $200 per share on Monday and it splits two for one on Tuesday, closing at $180, and then begins to trade at its split-adjusted price of around $90 on Wednesday, you'll find that on Wednesday your account will show a short position of 20 shares at around $90. When you buy to cover, you'll simply buy 20 shares. (Note that you should have a *very* good reason for shorting a stock just before it splits, since there is a strong trend for stock values to *rise* as a split approaches.)

Dividends

If the stock you sell short provides a dividend in any form—such as money or stock—while you're holding the short position, you will be required to return that dividend (that amount of money or stock) at the time you return the shares you borrowed. For example, let's say that you short 100 shares of Kanga Inc. While you're holding the position, Kanga, as a parent company, spins off its subsidiary Roo Corp. as a separately traded stock. The deal is that everyone who owns KNGA on a particular date will receive one share of ROOO for every ten shares of KNGA held. This means that since you have sold short 100 KNGA, then when you buy to cover, you must also buy 10 ROOO: one share of ROOO for every ten shares of KNGA you shorted.

TRADER TALK **Short interest** is the total number of shares of a stock that have been sold short and not yet repurchased. A large short interest means that there are many open short positions in the stock, and that a "short squeeze" is possible if the stock's price suddenly goes up. The short interest on listed stocks can be found at the Yahoo! Finance Web site and others, such as TrendFund.com.

TRADER TALK A **short squeeze** occurs when some event suddenly causes a stock price to rise, forcing many short sellers to buy to cover at the same time in an attempt to limit their losses. This sudden buying can accelerate the rise in price, causing even more short sellers to rush to buy to cover. A large short interest in a stock can make the effect of a short squeeze quite dramatic.

NEWBIE TRAP Avoid being caught in a short squeeze! If there is no compelling reason to be holding a short position, close it. If the stock has run out of downward momentum and there is no reason to think it will continue downward, it is very dangerous to continue to hold the position. Company news or another event could send the price up at any time, triggering a short squeeze.

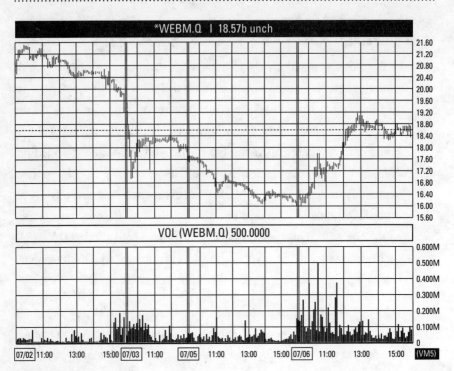

Short squeeze.
Chart provided by TradePortal.com, Inc.

WAXIE'S STREET SMARTS

Flexibility is one of the keys to long-term success in trading. After you've mastered the skill of making money in a down market by shorting, you can increase your flexibility even more by learning an advanced technique: options trading. Options can be played in a bull or bear market, and can be used to hedge your positions—to decrease your exposure if the market turns against you.

Exercises

Below are two possible short plays. One is a good short play, and the other is not. Consider all the information available, and decide which is the good play and which is the bad. What are the reasons for the good play? The reasons against the bad play?

I. BARK

The time is 12:30 P.M. The following information on Doggiestock.com has appeared today in Market Views on TrendFund.com:

10:32 ET *Mover Of Note*: Doggiestock.com (BARK) 6.93 (+1.42), volume 957K.

10:50 ET *Doggiestock.com (BARK)* 7.71 (+2.20):—**Update**—Stock reportedly up on favorable mention in the Hoohaw Technology Report.

11:05 ET *Hoohaw Report*: Doggiestock.com (BARK +2.29) was added to the Hoohaw "Telecosm" portfolio; Burnrate, Inc. (BURN – 6.5), HastaLaRasta (OMON −2.26) were reportedly removed due to competition from privately held Solidco.

The NASDAQ tanked immediately after trading opened today, and got as low as −52 at 10:45 A.M. Right now it's down about 35 points for the day.

You look at the five-day and thirty-day charts for BARK:

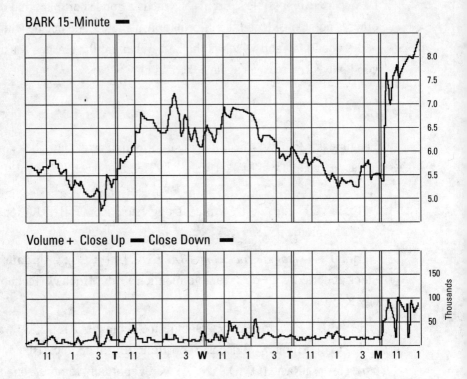

BARK 15-Minute ▬

The daily chart shows that BARK is now up 3.3 points for the day, as shown on the daily chart:

BARK Daily ▬ Earnings Up ▲ Down ▼ Dividends D

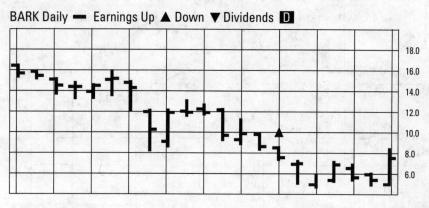

BARK 1-Minute ▬

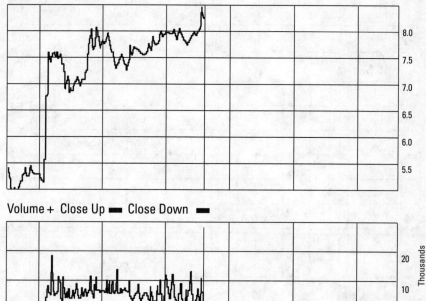

Volume + Close Up ▬ Close Down ▬

Should you short BARK at 8.3? What are the reasons for and against the play?

II. DREK

The time is 11:30 A.M. Digital Drek, Inc. (DREK) has been declining for months. Its fifty-two week high is 138, and its fifty-two-week low is 45.0. It is now trading at 55.0 an increase of 2.5 points from yes-

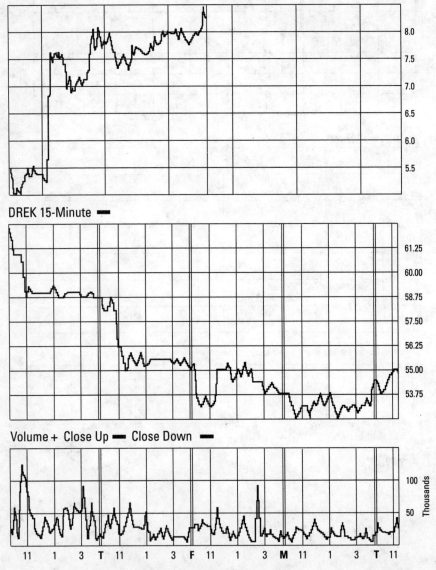

BARK 1-Minute

DREK 15-Minute

Volume + Close Up ━ Close Down ━

terday's low. You can see no reason for the gain—there is no news and the e-tailing sector is cold as a corpse. DREK is a weak company that has never turned a profit. The NASDAQ turned up when trading opened today, and is now up eighteen points for the day.

You look at the daily and five-day charts for DREK:

Should you short DREK at 55.0? What are the reasons for and against the play?

III. Discussion

BARK

Reasons in favor of shorting BARK:

- The market is *extremely* bearish.

- The stock has run up over 50 percent on news that does not seem extremely compelling. It has not been added to a major index, but merely to a little-known portfolio.

- The stock has been trending downward for at least the past month, suggesting weakness.

- The stock has just reached a new high for the day, suggesting that a retreat is likely—at least in the short term.

Reasons against shorting BARK:

- Uncertainty as to the long-term significance of the news.

DREK

Reasons in favor of shorting DREK:

- The price has gone up for no apparent reason.

- The stock has been trending downward for months and is generally weak.

Reasons against shorting DREK:

- The stock is trading in a range and has no significant momentum in either direction.

- General weakness in a stock is not by itself a good reason to short.

- There is no market weakness to drive the stock down.

- There is probably a large short interest in the stock, since it has been going down for months. Any news could cause a short squeeze.

- It is generally better to short a stock that has just run up too much, given the market climate, than to short a stock that does not have any momentum.

Outcomes

BARK

As shown by the chart below, BARK ended up dropping from 8.3 to 6.5. There were many compelling reasons to play this short, and with stops in place, it was a safe play that made sense.

The best way to play this short was to move your stop buy-to-cover order to progressively lower levels as the stock price moved down (this is known as using "trailing stops"). That way, if the stock turned back up, you would stop out of the position and preserve your profits. (As it happened, the stock did turn back up toward the end of the day, continued to go up the following day, and didn't stop until a few days after that.) By playing the short from 8.3 to 6.5, your return would be 1.8 points, or over 20 percent. Even if you set your last trailing stop at 7.0 and stopped out there when the stock turned back up, your return would be 1.3 points, or over 15 percent. Either way—*bingo ka-chingo*! And this was possible on a day when the NASDAQ was bleeding and bruised all day long.

BARK was a good short.

DREK 15-Minute ▬

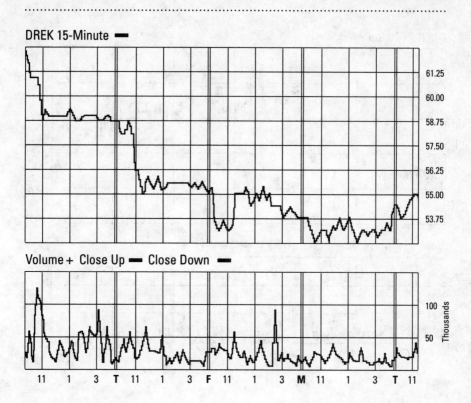

DREK

As shown in the chart below, the stock suddenly went up to 59.4 for no particular reason. Stocks that trade in a range often bounce up and down within their range. If you had shorted DREK at 55.0 and set a stop at five percent, you would have stopped out when the stock bounced to 59.4—a jump of almost 8 percent. When a stock has no momentum either up or down, random movements are certain to occur, and chances are great that you will soon stop out of a position as the price temporarily moves against you. As it happened, the stock move up to above 6 in the days that followed, before resuming its downward course.

DREK 1-Minute ━

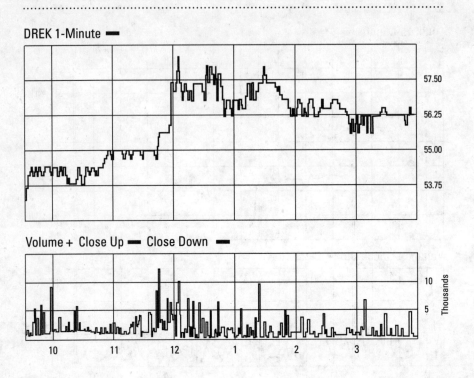

The bottom line is that there was absolutely no reason to believe that DREK would move down on this particular day. Therefore, there was no reason to short it. Making this kind of trade is like throwing darts to see where they'll land. You will never be a profitable trader if you take random positions without justification.

DREK was a bad short. It wasn't a disaster, but if you consistently stop out of poorly reasoned trades, each at a 5 percent loss, they will eventually eat up your entire account.

Chapter 11

Making It for Keeps

Six Keys to Sound Money Management

This chapter covers:
- Why capital preservation must be your first priority
- The two goals of good money management
- Six keys to sound money management
- Why failure to use safe trading and money-management practices is troubling risk-taking behavior

Protecting Your Capital Is Your First Priority

One of the toughest parts of being a successful trader is learning to be a good manager of your own money. It's completely possible—and actually pretty common—to see people turn out to be right on a high percentage of their stock picks *and still lose money*! How's that possible? If you don't use good money management by locking in profits, taking small losses on the picks you're wrong about, and controlling your use of margin, eventually you'll lose it all, no matter how good a stock picker you are.

As a trader, the most valuable thing you have is your capital. Without it, you can't trade at all—*it's all over*. Bringing in no profits at all is better than losing any part of your capital, because if your account is intact, you can always make a profit another day. If your capital has suffered a loss, you'll be wasting effort playing catch-up. The more you've lost, the longer it will take to get back to where you started from—both because you've got more to make up for, and also because with a smaller chunk of capital to work with, your profits for any given percentage return will be proportionally smaller. Making 10 percent on a $10,000 account earns you $1,000, but if you've lost half of that account and have only $5,000 left, making 10 percent on your money will earn you only $500. You'd have to do that twice to make the same $1,000.

Market corrections are inevitable, and will continue to occur from time to time. Traders must anticipate them and take precautions before they occur. Properly prepared, traders can even profit from corrections. Without proper money management, though, your account can be destroyed so quickly that your head will spin faster than Linda Blair's in *The Exorcist*.

The Two Goals of Good Money Management

Sound money management has two main goals: to *avoid losing money*, and to *avoid missing profit opportunities* by tying up capital in problem trades for long periods of time. Failing to avoid either of these will cost you a bundle.

Avoiding loss of money is pretty easy to understand: You want to preserve your capital and whatever profits you've accumulated. Not only do you want to keep it, but you want to trade with it as well, so that your capital continues to grow and makes your returns larger and larger.

Avoiding loss of profit opportunities isn't quite so obvious, but if you think about it, it's easy to see the point. Let's compare the outcomes of two money-management decisions. Trader A buys a stock, expecting it to go up, and finds that it doesn't. He's just sure it will go up eventually, and he's incurred a small loss, so he decides to wait it out. He ends up holding the stock for three months before finally selling it in disgust.

Trader B buys the same stock at the same time as Trader A, but once she sees that it isn't going up, she sells it at a small loss. She buys another stock and makes a 15 percent profit on it. Her next trade loses her 1 percent, but after that she makes 8 percent, 15 percent, and 30 percent on series of trades. Because she is growing her account, she makes these percentages on a larger and larger capital basis each time. At the end of three months, her account has grown by 48 percent.

Whose money-management decision turned out to be the best? If you chose Trader B, you win—a brand-new box of croutons! It's salad time. While Trader B made a nice profit, Trader A not only lost time but also never made his money back. Even if he had made his money back on that stock, it's hard to see how this was a good use of his capital over the course of three months.

Six Keys to Sound Money Management

There are six important things you must do to manage your account safely and effectively:

- Lock in profits
- Take small losses and make big gains
- Use margin with caution
- Go to cash when the market nears its top
- Diversify your portfolio
- Hedge risk

You must do these six things *consistently and without exception*. The most important difference *by far* between successful and unsuccessful traders is money management.

Exercising good money management is the single most important thing you can do to improve your trading performance.

Lock in profits

Lock them in or lose them. The choice is yours.

One of the most common and frustrating mistakes traders make is failing to lock in profits. It's all well and good to be up 35 percent on a trade, but it's only virtual money until you do something to *ensure* that it's yours to keep.

Remember the story of Mr. Loser? He watched his stocks go up initially, failed to take profits, and then watched them go back down—and down and down, until he'd actually lost money on what had been profitable positions. There's no reason this has to happen. It will happen, though, if you have no plan and no strategy for locking in profits.

How should you lock in profits? Since price targets are guidelines, something to be aimed at but not always hit right on the nose, I make a habit of selling half my shares at a more conservative target than the one I actually think the stock has a good chance of reaching. That way, I lock in a good chunk of profits, and whatever happens after that, there's no way *that* cash can disappear on me. Sometimes, if I think the stock could travel a long way, I plan several levels where I'll take profits—first selling half my position, then half of what's left, then half of what's left of that. Often these selling points are near psychological barriers I expect the stock to encounter—round numbers like 10, 20, and 50, or percentage barriers like a 25 percent gain for the day.

Another way I lock in profits is to use trailing stops. By continuously raising these stops as the stock price moves up, I lock in the profits I've made below the stops. I also protect the entire position in case of a sudden downturn.

These strategies must be part of the plan you have before you ever buy the stock. After you're in the position, it's too easy to get either panicked or carried away by high expectations. Locking in profits is part of your exit strategy and as such is part of the whole plan for the trade.

RULES OF THE GAME   Lock in profits religiously. *No one ever went broke taking profits!*

Let's look at a shorting example. You short Burnrate, Inc. at 38 after it runs up 100 percent in a day on modest news. You figure it could lose around half of its new gain in a day or so. You decide that you'll take half your profits when BURN gets down to about 35, another half when it reaches 32 or so, and the rest when it reaches the 29 area. You place a stop buy-to-cover order at 40.21 and settle down to wait.

Tank-o-rama! BURN is a burnout, and within an hour is approaching 35. You adjust your trailing stop to cover half your shares at a lower price and place a limit buy-to-cover order on the other half at 35.1, which executes. Ka-chingo!

Late in the day, the stock takes a dip down to 32.7, then 32.3. You know that a lot of people put in orders right at round numbers, so you always try to get in a little ahead of them. You buy to cover half of the shares you have left at 32.1. You reset your stop for a lower price on the shares that are left but let it expire at the end of the day because you think the stock might temporarily gap up in the morning as the last gasp of its big run. The stock closes at 32.6.

The next morning, the stock gaps up as you thought it might, reaching 33.4. It then starts to fall, slowly making its way toward your expected final selling point of just above 29. You reset your trailing stop at 33.6.

To your surprise, though, BURN picks up steam later in the morning and runs up to 33.9, triggering the stop on your remaining shares. It seems to have the legs to run for another day. You don't care, though—you're a happy dog, because you took profits at a much better price yesterday and no one can take them away from you. On top of that, you're now free to short BURN again once it reaches the top of its second-day run. Basically, you're relaxed and feeling dandy—you're even ready to do the Waxie jig! If you'd held your entire position, you'd have no profits and would have to wait for the stock to go down in order to see them—plus you'd run the risk of its going on a true rampage that could take it higher than the point where you shorted it.

Locking in profits is a beautiful, happy thing.

For examples of the use of trailing stops, take a look at Chapter 9.

Take small losses and make big gains

If you don't take small losses, you're gonna lose your butt.

I can't put it any more plainly than that. If you're unwilling to take a loss on any trade, I *guarantee* that you'll lose money.

Most people have trouble taking small losses. They don't want to lose anything on a trade because it makes them feel like they failed somehow. *But taking small losses means you succeeded!* Focus on the fact that you should take *small* losses, not that you should take *losses*. Taking *small* losses is a way to *limit* losses when they occur and to make sure they never turn into big ones. Taking small losses and big gains is the way successful traders trade. It's the only way to be a successful trader.

RULES OF THE GAME   Take small losses.

The best way to enforce the discipline of taking small losses is to *use protective stops on every trade*. If you decide how much you're willing to lose on a trade before you enter the position, as part of your plan, you can set your stop right after you enter the position and you won't have a chance to second-guess yourself. See Chapter 9 for a full discussion of stops.

RULES OF THE GAME   Always use stops.

If you think about how much you're willing to lose as part of your plan, it also helps you get real about whether the trade is one you really want to do in the first place. Taking a good look at your downside should do a lot to keep you away from questionable trades.

Use margin carefully

As discussed in Chapter 2, margin is a powerful tool that can really increase your profit but must always be used with care. The fact that using margin lets you make much more on successful trades but lose much more on unsuccessful trades should make you even more carefully evaluate the risk-to-reward ratio every time you look at a potential trade.

What's the proper way to use margin?

First of all, don't use *all* of it. Always leave yourself a generous cushion. Every change in the price of a stock in your portfolio changes the value of the collateral you have available for your margin loan. If the value of your holdings goes down, it will go down faster due to margin than if you weren't using margin, and this means that the size of your margin cushion will decrease at the same faster rate. I suggest that you never use more than two-thirds of your total margin capacity. This leaves at least one-third as a cushion. If declining stock values bring your cushion to below one-third of your capacity, it may be time to sell some shares to keep you out of trouble.

Second, when deciding how great a loss you can tolerate on any one trade, remember to take margin into account. If you're using half your margin capacity, a 2 percent loss on the value of a stock position will equal a 3 percent loss to your actual capital.

Learn how your broker calculates account equity. This can be very confusing, but it's really helpful to be able to anticipate how much margin capacity you'll be left with after you make a trade. Always keep track of your margin status. Check it every morning and at the end of every trading day.

Don't worry about margin interest. Your broker will charge interest on the borrowed amount, but the interest rate is low and the cost is trivial if you're trading profitably.

In general, use margin only in markets with a strong bullish direction. You can't use margin capacity to increase the sizes of short positions in a bear market, anyway (though you must have a margin account to short). Whenever the market seems overbought, unsteady, or unclear in its direction, get completely out of margin before a downturn can take place.

Go to cash when the market nears its top

Besides getting out of margin when the market seems unsteady or overbought, you should also lighten up on stock positions and go mostly to cash. When the market is about to turn, *cash is king*! Staying away from unpredictable and untradable volatility will save your account from potentially devastating losses. You'll be smiling when things finally calm down and you have lots of fresh cash to trade with while others are still licking their wounds.

Diversify your portfolio

As discussed in Chapter 2, diversification is very important in trading. Putting all of your money into positions that carry the same types of risk is not good money management. Instead, find trades with different risks so that if one sector experiences a sudden downturn, only a portion of your account will be affected.

Hedge risk

Learn about strategies for hedging risk. For example, if you're playing a stock that you believe will go up but could instead go down, try to find a weaker stock that should generally go in the same direction and short it. That way, if the primary stock goes down, you'll profit from your short, which is likely to fall faster because it's weaker. If it doesn't fall, it's not likely to rise as fast for the same reason.

Many common hedging strategies involve options. Two examples, straddles and strangles, are outside the scope of this book, but it makes sense to learn about them.

TRADER TALK   A *straddle* is an options play where both a call and a put are purchased. The call and put have the same strike price, the same expiration month, and the same underlying stock or index.

TRADER TALK   A *strangle* is an options play where both a call and a put are purchased. The call and put have different strike prices (usually both out of the money), but have the same expiration month and the same underlying stock or index.

Hedging is a form of insurance, so it will cost you a bit by decreasing the profits you make on a play. But there are times when insurance is well worth the cost.

Risk-taking As a Form of Escapism

Traders who routinely fail to use safe trading and money-management practices should ask themselves *why* they're engaging in dangerous and self-defeating behavior. There's always a psychological motivation for something that doesn't otherwise make sense. What are they getting out of it, since it's clear that they're not getting better financial results?

Risky behavior is often a form of escapism or a substitute for something more meaningful in a person's life. If you seem to resist using proper money management or often "forget" to make a plan or set stops, take a look at your own motivations. Better to figure it out now, deal with it, and prosper than to lose all your money because you didn't know what you were really trying to do.

WAXIE'S STREET SMARTS

If you find yourself taking unnecessary risks or engaging in other self-injurious behavior, try to figure out your subconscious or unconscious motivations and deal with them in the light of day.

Chapter 12

Keeping Your Edge

The Rules of the Game

This chapter covers:

- Why you must commit to following the Rules of the Game
- How to keep all the Rules of the Game in mind while you trade

The Rules of the Game (a.k.a. Essential Principles of Good Trading)

Here are the most important rules I follow to make me a successful trader. I don't usually like to lay down hard-and-fast rules, both because it sounds too authoritarian and because I know that every rule has an exception and that different things work for different people. That's why this list doesn't contain rules about things that may be appropriate for traders with one style but not for traders with other styles—things like the trends I like to play, or the way I like to structure my trading day. Instead, these are the rules that have to do with the discipline a good trader *must have* to become and remain a winner. Think of them as *essential principles of good trading*.

Take this page of rules out of the book and tape it up right beside your computer screen. I'm completely serious about this. I want you to have these rules in your head *at all times* while you're trading.

Once you become a confident trader, you may discover other rules or principles that work for you. When you do, follow them as consistently as you follow these. Some of them are pretty good rules for life, too—you may find them coming in handy when you least expect it. That's how life is: If you're open to the gifts it has to offer and allow yourself to receive them, there's no telling how rich—in every sense—they can make you.

PICKING A STOCK	PLAYING A STOCK	PLAYING TO WIN
Always have a good reason. *No reason, no play!*	Plan the trade and trade the plan.	Play to win!
Don't play maybes. *When in doubt, stay out!*	Don't buy the gap up.	Be open.
Most tips don't pan out.	Don't chase a stock; wait for it to come to you. *Last one in the pool swims with the turd!*	You don't need to win on every trade.
Trends are your friends.	Buy the rumor, sell the news.	No one makes money every day.
Go for the easy money. *Think in terms of risk/reward!*	Always use stops.	It's a marathon, not a sprint.
Don't catch falling knives.	Lock in profits religiously. *No one ever went broke taking profits!*	Be flexible. *Don't fight the market! Don't fight the trend!*
	Greed = Death. *Pigs get slaughtered!*	On a bad day, take a walk.
	Swing for singles, not the fences—and often you'll hit home runs anyway.	Control your inner knucklehead.
	Take small losses.	Use sound money management.
	Don't marry stocks.	You are responsible for everything you do, both in trading and in life. *There are no victims, only volunteers!*
	Don't panic buy or panic sell.	You don't have to trade every day.
		Make trading fun.
		Remember to give something back.
		Have a life outside trading.
Rule the freakin' markets!	*Rule the freakin' markets!*	*Rule the freakin' markets!*

Chapter 13

The Pursuit of Wowsa!

Trading to Follow Your Dreams

- Why trading should be the means to an end, not an end in itself
- Why you must focus on what's most important in your life and always pursue your dreams
- Why it's important to examine your priorities
- How good trading teaches valuable lessons you can use in other areas of your life
- Principles for living that will bring a *Wowsa!* to your life every day and also help make you a winning trader

The Pursuit of Wowsa!

Why are you trading?

That question isn't as simple as it might seem. The obvious answer, the one you might expect from everyone, is, "Well, *duh*—for the money, what else?"

But what's the money *for*? *What's your ultimate goal?* This is a question everyone needs to think about, and one some people never get around to asking themselves.

Let me tell you why I trade, and maybe my reasons will help you think more about your own.

I trade as the means to an end. I don't do it because it's what I've always wanted to do, and trading still isn't the only thing I want to do. The reason I started trading stocks in the first place was to pursue my dream, which is to write and direct films. I want to make movies—my own movies, movies that are real and true, movies that will speak to others and offer them something of value. I want to do this without relying on anyone else for funding because, as any screenwriter will tell you, even if someone in Hollywood buys your script, there's no guarantee that they'll ever make your film—or, if they do, that they'll do it right.

I've already made a short film that was shown at numerous festivals, written several screenplays that were optioned, and been a finalist three times for the Sundance Institute's Screenwriting and Filmmaking Laboratories. I've also won several playwriting awards, and there have been over twenty productions of my plays. I tell you this only to show how much my dream means to me. Making a film is something that will truly make me go, *Wowsa!* My hope is that you're also trading as the means to some greater end in your life, some important goal that's meaningful, lasting, and real. I believe that your ultimate trading goal should be to get to a place where you feel a bigger *Wowsa!* and sense of satisfaction about your life than you felt after your most awesome winning trade. Never give up on your dreams. Instead, do whatever you have to do to make them come true.

What are your most cherished dreams? What's the most important thing in your life?

WAXIE'S STREET SMARTS

Never give up on your dreams.

Remember, too, that trading isn't the only path to achieving your dreams. You may eventually find another path that better suits your situation and who you are. Some will make a fortune trading, and in that way will change their lives. Many already have. Others will not be able to, for whatever reason. Those who don't may be tempted to blame themselves or others. It's not their fault or anyone else's—it just means trading isn't their road. They have to keep traveling. There are always other roads.

For some people, though, trading isn't even about the money, much less about a dream. For those people, trading is an end in itself—the activity is the final goal. In fact, I've met people whose lives have come to revolve around trading. They're looking for action, something to focus on, something to care about. Some of them are lonely and isolated from life outside cyberspace. For them, trading has become an escape from life.

What are your real reasons for trading? Do you feel that you need to trade every day? Trading, like just about anything else, can become a form of addiction for some people. If you ever find that trading has replaced other parts of your life or become an end in itself, please stop, step back, and take an honest look at your priorities. *What's really important to you? How can you achieve it?* Think hard about these questions from time to time. Trading should never take the place of meaningful goals and relationships in your life. Make sure trading is the means to a worthy end—not an end in itself.

What Trading Can Teach You About Life

Instead of replacing life, trading should teach you some important lessons that can help you live it well. The rules and discipline of trading aren't so different from some of the principles that shape successful lives.

What are they?

1. Exercise self-discipline.

People who are successful in any area of life, whether it's trading, a profession, athletics, or relationships, are able to focus on a goal and do whatever they need to do to reach it. This often means refusing to take the easy approach, resisting impulses, bypassing opportunities for instant gratification, making yourself do things that aren't necessarily fun, and adhering to a routine or a plan. It's all about taking responsibility for the direction your pursuits will take.

RULES OF THE GAME   You are responsible for everything you do, both in trading and in life. *There are no victims, only volunteers!*

2. Approach life as a marathon, not a sprint.

Success requires perseverance over a long period of time, not short bursts of effort every now and then. Any large undertaking is best approached this way. You won't get rich after a week of trading, and if you try, you'll end up losing your money by taking excessive risks. Instead, bring in profits steadily and watch your success grow week by week, month by month.

RULES OF THE GAME   It's a marathon, not a sprint.

3. Learn continuously.

Things keep changing, in the market and everywhere else in the world. You have to keep up. This means never becoming married to one strategy, one stock, or one explanation. It also means keeping an open mind to new ideas and new information when they're offered to you, and actively seeking them out when they aren't.

RULES OF THE GAME   Be open.

4. Maintain a winning attitude.

People who expect to lose rarely win. They don't believe there's any use in trying, so they don't put forth the effort necessary to succeed. People who expect to win believe in themselves enough to do whatever they need to do to win. *If you're going to play at all, play to win!*

RULES OF THE GAME   Play to win.

Make All Paths Lead to *Wowsa!*

Just as the lessons of trading can help you in the rest of your life, the way you live your life can improve your trading tremendously. Here are the things that bring the *Wowsa!* to my life every day and help make me a successful trader and a successful person. They really boil down to two things, which are intimately related: being good to others and being good to yourself.

1. Be good to others.

For me, there's no joy in a selfish existence that tries to take more than it gives. I want to be good to others because it makes me feel good, not because I think I have to or because I'm trying to get something from them. Try it yourself. Be kind and generous with no strings attached. It will make you feel very good and very free.

2. Give something back.

One of the most important things I've been able to do by becoming a successful trader is to give money to charity, and to encourage others to do the same.

When I was a kid, I was so angry that I was constantly getting into fights. The kids I fought with were usually much older than me. I lost a lot of fights, but since I was always the underdog, I made it a point never to pick on anyone smaller than I was. I wanted a fight to be fair, or else for me to have to reach up to win.

That's the way I feel about trading, too. I swore to myself long ago that one day, when I was making enough money to live my dreams, I'd help every underdog I possibly could.

That's why giving to charity is so important to me.

Besides my dream of making films, my motivation in trading and teaching others to trade well is simply to level the playing field. I want to make sure that everyone has an equal shot at winning—that in the end, no matter what each of us has gone through, we can all reach our goals.

I believe in the paradox that you can't keep your wealth unless you give it back. It's a spiritual axiom that you'll get back twelve times as much as you give to others. Please keep that in mind. In a sense, being charitable is actually selfish, because in the end you'll get back much more than you've given. But charity is a spiritually healthy kind of selfishness.

RULES OF THE GAME Remember to give something back.

3. Live a physically healthy life.

One important way to be good to yourself is to stay healthy. Not taking care of yourself is a subtle form of self-punishment. If you're pursuing your dreams, you've got a lot to live for. You should feel good while you're doing it!

I try to eat right (if you love sushi as much as I do, how could you go wrong?) and to seek out things that are good for me. I drink my green juice and my carrot-beet juice every day and take the vitamins I need. I exercise to keep myself strong, because a ninja can't become weak. Exercise is also a great way to relieve stress, and being relaxed makes me a better trader. I sleep as much as I can, though that's something I'm still working on. I stay away from things that will hurt me, and I try not to stress out over little things.

Feeling good makes you feel like a winner, and if you feel like a winner, you're much more likely to be one—both in trading and in life.

4. Live a spiritually healthy life.

What is spiritual health? I believe that it means being conscious—aware—of yourself and how you affect other people, of reality and what's going on in the world. It's being aware of what it is that we're all striving for, everyone in his or her own way. Everyone is striving for happiness, in whatever form it might take in their personal vision. They're trying to achieve harmony. To me, achieving happiness means getting back to the place of innocence and love we were born into, before the world started to hurt us and make us angry and cynical and afraid. For me, happiness means being free and able to accomplish what I want to accomplish without anyone saying I can't because I'm not good enough.

My life's been neither easy nor simple, and I still struggle with many things. You don't have experiences like the ones I've had without needing to battle some old demons later on. But I've gotten a lot of guidance, and I've learned the value of spiritual health. I know that if I accept my life's challenges head-on, stay aware, and accept responsibility for my actions, I can choose my destiny.

5. Eat well.

This one is really important to me. There were lots of times earlier in my life when I went hungry because I didn't have enough money. At some point, I promised myself that I would never go hungry again, and that no matter what else I lacked, I would always eat well.

So now I do. I treat myself to sushi at least twice a week, and I eat other food I like that's healthful and nutritious. I don't eat red meat, and I don't eat anything else I don't want to eat.

Eating well is all part of feeling good and being in top form for whatever you've set out to do. It's all part of playing to win.

6. Have fun.

If there's no joy in what you're doing, there's no point in doing it. You won't do it well, and life's too short to spend doing something you hate. Do what you can to make trading fun. I put on my black ninja underwear, crank up some stellar tunes, and shout out loud when I make a good trade. If the trade's *really* good, I'll even do the Waxie jig. Now, *that's* having *fun*, baby!

Don't get so serious about trading that you can't enjoy it. Chat and joke around with other traders, amuse yourself, and never take yourself too seriously. All this has definitely worked for me!

RULES OF THE GAME   Make trading fun.

7. Feel comfortable about making money.

It's funny: You'd think that after growing up without any money, successful people would be so happy and relieved that they'd just put the past behind them, forget being poor, and enjoy the gifts they were given. I can tell you from experience that that's hard to do. The memories are always part of you.

That can be okay, though. My memories keep me grateful, honest, and diligent about making the playing field level, and they keep me trying to help others find the good things I've found.

Memories may be okay, but guilt isn't. Some people find that winning makes them feel guilty, as though they don't deserve success or are taking something from someone else.

This guilt is misplaced and harmful. Don't let guilt ruin your success. It's okay to succeed! Winning is a good, good thing. You'll have worked hard for it, and you deserve it. It's yours and is meant to be yours. If you use your success wisely, remember to give something back, and help others achieve their own success, there's nothing to feel guilty about. Your success is a gift you can pass on to other people. If you use it for good, what is there to feel bad about?

8. Have a life outside trading.

Remember, *trading is only a means to an end*. The end is somewhere else in your life. Trading is supposed to make your life better, not take it over. Hang out with friends, take vacations, do things you enjoy, and care for your significant other and your loved ones. If you don't have a significant other, maybe it's time to get one!

RULES OF THE GAME   Have a life outside trading.

See You on the Other Side!

I've been able to transform my life from a state of unhappiness and want into a completely different existence—as though I passed through a long, dark, horrific tunnel and finally came out into the daylight on the other side. Maybe you'll relate to some of the things I've been through, and maybe the fact that I've managed to come out on the other side—and end up where I have—will inspire you to keep following your dreams. I hope so.

I was born in New York City. When I was four years old, right after my brother was born, my father left us. I haven't seen him since, and he never gave my mother a cent in child support. My mother worked three jobs, received food stamps and welfare, and couldn't afford day care, so at four I was in charge of looking after my baby brother while my mother worked and struggled to make ends meet. Things got so bad that one day my mother came home and found me covered with roaches. They were crawling over every part of my body. My mother, hysterical, rushed me to the hospital, and the doctor told her that if she hadn't made it home right when she did, I would have suffocated and died. As it was, I had a rash for a month.

I grew up poor, and for a long time I had a massive chip on my shoulder. When I was a teenager, it seemed that my true destiny was to die on the streets. I came close many, many times. I had guns held to my head and was close to starvation more than once. I've also been lucky, though. I'm truly blessed to be alive, since that was none of my doing. I saw many less fortunate friends die along that old road.

I'm still kind of hard and tough, but it's nothing compared to the way I was when I was younger. I've stopped feeling so angry about my upbringing now. I've been through uglier stuff than most people would go through in ten lifetimes and I wouldn't wish any of it on anyone, but in spite of that, I don't assume that my life has been worse than anyone else's. That's because I know that, whatever our color or background, we all have our demons and all suffer at times. We each travel a different road, but all of them have dark tunnels we have to pass through.

Except for my memories, my hard past is behind me now. I've emerged from my tunnel to sit in the sunshine, and the next tunnel I'm facing isn't nearly as long or as terrible. It's all about writing scripts and making movies, and believe me, I've got the material ready and waiting.

I'll bet right now you're working your way through a dark tunnel on your own road. You can't wait to emerge into the light on the other side, and you're looking for a way to move forward toward it. If you keep going, you'll find the place where I am now, whether you do it by becoming a successful trader or by succeeding in another way. In the end, you'll meet me on the other side.

I hope to see you there.

Good Luck!

I sincerely wish you the best possible success in the market—and, even more importantly, in life! I hope my story and the knowledge I've gained during my education in trading will inspire you to follow your dreams and eventually achieve them, whether through trading—*making your ka-chingos for keeps!*—or by taking another path. There's no single right way to find the *Wowsa!* in life; the only thing that matters is that you don't give up on the quest. I hope that, no matter what the means (as long as they don't involve using or hurting others), you will succeed in changing your life into whatever you want it to be.

WAXIE'S STREET SMARTS
Always follow your dreams. Don't ever give up on them!

Best wishes, and the best of success in making your dreams come true!

Michael Parness is the owner of one of the largest financial Web sites, and his infomercial *www.trendtradingtowin.com* has sold over 150,000 tapes to clients around the world. His new book, *Power Trading/Power Living* is just about completed. He recently wrote and directed his first feature film, *Max and Grace* (www.maxandgrace.com), and his rags to riches life story was optioned by Dustin Hoffman. Michael has also been honored at the United Nations for his charity work with children. He lives in New York City.

Glossary

An excellent source of additional trading-term definitions is at www.trendfund. com. There's also a glossary of over 5,000 words at www.investorwords.com.

A/D   The ratio of advancers to decliners, which serves as a breadth analysis indicator.

Ask   The price at which a seller will sell a stock. Also known as the *offer*. The *best ask* is the lowest quoted price at which a seller will sell a stock at a particular time.

Ax   A market maker with a large order to fill who is moving the stock price aggressively.

Bearish   Pessimistic; expecting the market to go down or a stock's price to fall.

Bid   The price at which a buyer will buy a stock. The *best bid* is the highest quoted price at which a buyer will buy a stock at a particular time.

Blue sky   A new fifty-two-week high. In blue sky, the stock has no known resistance to hold it back.

Bollinger bands   An indicator used in price charting which uses past data and standard deviations to show support and resistance.

Bounce   A sudden upward price movement that follows a downtrend and may or may not signal a larger change in direction.

Breakout   A new high for the day, or a stock's departure from an established range.

Bullish   Optimistic; expecting the market to go up or a stock's price to rise.

Buy to cover   To close a short-scale position by purchasing shares to replace the shares borrowed by the account. See *sell short*.

Call   An option to buy a stock at a future date at a specific price. Compare *put*.

Dead cat bounce A *bounce* that does not signal a change in direction from downtrend to uptrend or rally; instead, a dead cat bounce is merely a brief interruption in a strong downtrend.

Dow Jones Industrial Average (DJIA) The thirty largest industrial stocks, used as an index.

Downtick A lowered bid. You cannot sell short on a downtick.

Electronic communications network (ECN) A computerized exchange system that makes market makers' and other parties' orders available for execution by third parties.

Ex-date The day a stock's share price changes to reflect a stock split and revised number of shares are credited to shareholders' accounts.

Fading the gap Going against the initial morning NASDAQ gap, or generally playing off an imbalance.

Gap down A significant price move down from the previous day's close.

Gap up A significant price move up from the previous day's close.

High of the day The highest price at which a particular stock has been traded on a given day.

Hitting the bid Using a limit sell order equal to the bid in order to get out of a position quickly.

Home run An incredible return on one trade, such as 40 percent, 75 percent, or 100 percent. Compare *single*.

INCA Level II abbreviation for the Instinet ECN, a favorite hiding place where market makers and other large buyers and sellers trade when they don't want their identities to be known.

Initial public offering (IPO) The first time a company sells stock to the public.

Intraday Inside a single trading day.

ISLD Level II abbreviation for the Island ECN.

IPO See *initial public offering.*

Ka-chingo! A nice profit on a good trade.

Level I A basic stock-quotation system showing only the current best bid and ask prices and order sizes, along with information on the last executed trade.

Level II A real-time streaming stock quotation system showing all market makers' and ECNs' posted bid and ask prices and order sizes.

Level III   A NASDAQ order desk for market makers, not available to individual traders.

Limit order   An order that can execute only at the stated price or better. Check with your broker; some brokers use slightly different names for various order types.

Liquidity   The ability of a stock or other security to be converted into cash quickly and without incurring a loss. The easier the conversion is, the more *liquid* the stock; if conversion is difficult, the stock is *illiquid*. Markets often achieve liquidity by having a large number of buyers and sellers.

Listed stocks   Stocks that are traded on an exchange such as the NYSE or AMEX, as opposed to over-the-counter stocks.

Lockup expiration   Date on which IPO shares that insiders bought can be sold on the open market.

Lot   A number of shares of the same stock that are traded or held together. Level I quotes show only lots of 100 (*round lots*), but a lot of any size may be traded (lots that are not multiples of 100 are called *odd lots*).

Low of the day   The lowest price at which a particular stock has been traded on a given day.

Margin   The capacity to borrow against the securities in your account. *Buying on margin* means using the shares you hold long as collateral to borrow money to buy more stock.

Margin call   A broker's notification to an account holder to sell securities or deposit funds in order to meet a margin requirement. If the account holder takes no action, the broker will liquidate holdings.

Market maker (MM)   A firm authorized to buy and sell securities on an exchange at publicly quoted bid and ask prices.

Market order   An order to sell a security at market price, which equals best bid when selling and best ask when buying.

Momentum (momo)   The strength (due to volume) of the buying or selling that's causing a stock's price to move. When a price movement has momentum behind it, the movement is more likely to continue in the same direction, at least in the short term.

NASD   National Association of Securities Dealers.

NASDAQ   National Association of Securities Dealers Automated Quotation system.

....

Newbie   A new, inexperienced trader.

NYSE   New York Stock Exchange.

Odd lot   A stock holding or order to buy stock in a quantity that is not a multiple of 100. See *lot*.

Option   A contract giving the owner the right but not the obligation to purchase (call) or sell short (put) a stock at a particular price by a specified date.

Price chart   The main tool used in technical analysis, in which price movement is charted over time on *x* and *y* axes.

Pump-and-dump scheme   A stock manipulation in which the stock's price is made to rise dramatically ("pumped") by rumor or hype so that the manipulators can sell ("dump") their shares at the inflated price before it collapses.

Put   An option to sell short a security at a future date at a predetermined price. Compare *call*.

Quiet period   A twenty-five-day period after a company's stock has gone public (after an IPO has started trading), during which neither the company nor its underwriters issue any news on the company.

Resistance   A price level at which a stock has previously reversed its upward course.

Rinse   A sharp spike down for no apparent reason. Market makers are suspected of creating such movements in order to trigger stop orders.

Risk-to-reward ratio   The comparison or relative size of a trade's anticipated risk to its anticipated reward.

Round lot   A quantity of shares of a stock held or ordered that is a multiple of 100. See *lot*.

S&P 500   Standard and Poor's 500 index. An index of 500 of the largest stocks in the marketplace.

Scalp   A quick trade, lasting a few minutes, for a small profit.

Sector   A subset of the market whose component companies are in the same general area of business.

Sell short ("short")   To sell a security you do not own in order to make money on a downward price movement. Compare *take long*.

Short squeeze   A sharp move upward, causing short sellers to buy to cover.

Single   A respectable return on one trade, such as 3 percent, 5 percent, or 8 percent. Compare *home run*.

Size   The number of one-hundred-share blocks available at the bid or ask.

SOES   Small Order Execution System. It give users the ability to make a NASDAQ market maker take your small order regardless of the size the market maker is advertising. The maximum size allowed varies by security.

Specialist   A single person responsible for all trades in a single stock. NYSE and AMEX use specialists.

SPOOS   Standard & Poor's 500 index futures, which is often used as a market indicator.

Spread   The difference between the bid and ask.

Stop order   A *stop-loss order*.

Stop limit order   An order to sell a stock *at a specific price and no lower than that price* if it drops to that price, or to buy to cover a stock sold short *at a specific price and no higher than that price* if it rises to that price. Once the stop is triggered, the order is executed *only* if it can be executed at the limit price or better (it becomes a limit order). Check with your broker; some brokers use slightly different names for various order types.

Stop-loss order   An order to sell a stock if it drops to a specified price, or to buy to cover a stock you sold short if it rises to a specified price. Once the stop is triggered, the order is executed *immediately* at the market price (it becomes a market order). Check with your broker; some brokers use slightly different names for various order types.

Straddle   An options play where both a call and a put are purchased. The call and put have the same strike price, the same expiration month and the same underlying stock or index.

Strangle   An options play where both a call and a put are purchased. The call and put have different strike prices (usually both out of the money), but have the same expiration month and the same underlying stock or index.

Super Dot   The electronic order execution system for NYSE stocks.

Support   A price level at which a stock has previously bounced (reversed its downward course).

Take long   To buy a stock. Compare *sell short*.

Trend   A price movement pattern that is repeated by different stocks and can be relied on to reasonably anticipate the price movements of similar stocks.

U/D or UD   The ratio between the advancing volume and the declining volume, which serves as a directional strength indicator.

Uptick   A raised bid. An uptick allows a short sale to occur.

Volatility   The degree to which a stock's price moves up and down. A highly volatile stock experiences large price fluctuations, while a more stable stock does not. A particular stock's volatility can vary over time according to market and stock-specific conditions.